The BHSAI Course Companion

THE BHSAI COURSE
COMPANION

by

JO FRENCH, BHSAI

J. A. ALLEN
London

British Library Cataloguing in Publication Data
French, Jo
    The B.H.S.A.I. course companion.
    1. Great Britain. Livestock: Horses. Riding. Instructors
    I. Title
    798.23076

    ISBN 0–85131–500–3

Published in Great Britain in 1990 by
J. A. Allen & Company Limited,
1, Lower Grosvenor Place, Buckingham Palace Road,
London, SW1W 0EL

Printed in Hong Kong by Dah Hua Printing Co., Ltd.

Contents

For Coral

List of Illustrations

Acknowledgements

I am indebted to Captain Elwyn Hartley Edwards for his invaluable advice during the editing stage of this book and whose experience has undoubtedly improved it considerably.

Thanks are also due to Maggie Raynor who speedily produced the excellent line drawings to exacting instructions.

Finally to Mike whose help and support carried the project through to completion.

Foreword

There is a list of books recommended by the British Horse Society as reading for the Assistant Instructor's Certificate. Without doubt these books provide a valuable basis of background knowledge, but none have been written specifically for the examination and none are devoted to it exclusively.

This manual does not presume to replace anything on the recommended list. Instead, its purpose is to complement existing material whilst presenting a comprehensive summary of the syllabus requirements within a single volume.

It cannot, of course, take the place of sound, practical training which is the basis of the Assistant Instructor's Certificate, but it is hoped that it provides a key to the underlying theory, as well as guidelines on the way the various aspects of the examination are best approached.

Jo French
Knebworth, 1989

1   Background and Training

The Examination Structure

The British Horse Society defines its examinations as follows:

The examination for the BHSAI consists of two parts — the Horse Knowledge and Riding Stage III (which replaced the Horsemaster's Certificate in January 1986) and the Preliminary Teaching Test.

Each is an entirely separate exam and can be taken on its own but qualification for the full BHSAI Certificate requires that both exams are passed. Candidates who pass the HK & R Stage III are eligible to take the HK & R Stage IV and those passing the BHSAI are eligible to take the Intermediate Teaching Test. These two exams together make up the British Horse Society Intermediate Instructor's Certificate, which is the next step up from the BHSAI.

Following the BHSII is the Instructor's exam (BHSI) which consists of three parts — the Stable Manager's Certificate, the Equitation Certificate and the Teaching Certificate, each of which is taken separately, although the Stable Manager's Certificate is a prerequisite for the other two.

The highest qualification is the Fellowship (FBHS) which requires an extremely high level of ability in all spheres. The minimum age for entry to this exam is 25 years.

The Horse Knowledge and Riding Stage III Examination

Eligibility — BHS members of 17 years and over

Prerequisites — HK & R Stages I & II. (Note that HK & R Stage II has the prerequisite of the BHS Riding and Road Safety Test.)

Requirements — The candidate must show an ability to look after up to

1

four horses in stables and at grass and to ride a variety of well-mannered horses under a variety of circumstances. He should be tactful yet effective, understanding the reasons for his actions both in horse care and while riding.

Syllabus HORSE KNOWLEDGE AND CARE

General — An increase of responsibility; looking after a small number of horses and ponies (up to four) with less supervision; ensuring that horses, stable yard and fields are safe and in good order.

Horse Psychology — Knowledge of the horse's natural lifestyle, instincts, actions and reactions. Know the value of calmness and kindness in establishing the horse's confidence and improving his well-being and therefore his work.

Horse Physiology — Knowledge of the use of the horse's main trunk muscles to move his limbs and to support and carry his rider. Basic outline of horse's respiratory and circulatory systems. Good and bad conformation.

Horse Health — Take and record temperature, pulse and respiration and treat minor injuries, minor ailments, sickness and lameness; how to prevent them and when to call the veterinary surgeon and what information to give. Administer medicines in food, water or by oral syringe. Knowledge of worming procedures.

Management and General Handling — Ability to take charge of several horses and ponies in stables and at grass. Some knowledge of dealing with young, highly strung or problem horses, including those with stable vices. Preparing and looking after fit horses; preparation of horses for the show-ring and competition. Knowledge of procedures when travelling by trailer or horsebox and for loading and unloading. Lungeing an experienced horse efficiently in an enclosed space. Demonstrate knowledge and ability to take horses on ride and lead exercise in a competent manner.

Feeding — Ability to monitor and organise the feed-store and to plan feed-charts to suit individual requirements, e.g. for children's ponies, young horses, hunters, "hot" or sluggish horses. An understanding of the value of grass and concentrates and of the significance of carbohydrates, proteins, fats and oils, minerals, vitamins, fibre and water in the horse's diet.

Saddlery — Organising a saddle room; care of its contents. Cleaning and storage of saddlery. The correct principles and fitting of saddlery and bits in general use, including those used for training young horses, competition work and for problem horses.

Clothing — Putting on sweat sheets and exercise bandages. Cleaning and storage of clothing.

Shoeing — What to look for in a newly shod foot. Special shoes for special cases, e.g. plain, hunter, rolled-toe, feather-edged, three-quarter, grass-tips. Use of foot-pads and studs. Faulty shoeing and consequential ill-effects.

Action — The sequence of footfalls at all gaits; good and faulty action and the terms used to describe these.

Stable Design — Understanding of simple planning of the stable yard and of the advantages and disadvantages of different types of stabling and of fittings.

Grassland Management

Syllabus RIDING

Effective yet sympathetic riding, while maintaining a balanced, correct and supple seat at all gaits and when jumping fences up to 0.9 metres (3 ft). Knowledge of school figures.

Correct influences and smooth application of the aids with a clear understanding of the reasons for them.

Riding horses forward with a good form through transitions, lengthening and shortening of strides at all gaits, turns on the forehand, leg-yielding, quarter pirouettes and the rein back (two or three steps).

Ability to ride with or without stirrups and with the reins in one or both hands, in a snaffle or a double bridle.

Understanding of the value of school work in the mental, muscular and gymnastic development of the horse.

Practical and theoretical knowledge of the methods and primary concerns when getting horses fit for regular work and for novice competitions. Knowledge of the rules of riding at competitive and social events.

Good judgement of pace and distance at walk, trot and canter. Riding and jumping out of doors over a variety of fences and terrain.

Syllabus   GENERAL KNOWLEDGE

Know the risks and responsibilities involved when riding on the public
  highway. Correct procedures in the event of accidents. Safety
  rules and fire precautions in the stable yard.

The Preliminary Teaching Test

Eligibility — BHS members who have reached the age of 17½ years
  and over who hold four 'O' levels at grade A, B or C (or CSE
  grade 1) or their equivalents, one of which must be in English
  Language or English Literature. Candidates who have reached
  the age of 19 will be allowed exemption from this academic
  qualification.

Prerequisites — HK & R Stage II

Requirements — Candidates must show that they have the required
  qualities, and can apply the basic principles of teaching, e.g.
  manner, voice, control etc, and that they have the ability to
  improve their pupil's horsemanship and horsemastership
  with a progressive plan.
      They must know the procedure and principles with regard
  to safety in the stage organisation of a lesson or hack (in the
  open country or on the roads).
      They must have a knowledge of how to proceed should
  there be an accident or an emergency, and have a sound
  knowledge of road safety.

Syllabus   TEACHING

Take a lesson of three or four pupils who are at HK & R Stage II level
  and working for Stage III. Show ability to assess pupils and
  give a constructive class lesson on the flat, including the use
  of ground poles, or give an early jumping lesson.
      Show a sound knowledge of basic equitation and be able to
  give clear explanations of lesson subjects and teaching format
  for the standard indicated above.
      Give a lead rein lesson suitable for a complete beginner or a
  lunge lesson suitable for a novice adult or child rider.

Give oral/practical stable lecturettes of up to five minutes, suitable for HK & R Stage II, Riding Club Grade II or Pony Club C Test standard candidates. Answer simple questions on safety and accident procedure.

Note: candidates may be required to give these lessons in the open and/or in a covered school. Ground poles, cavalletti or small jumps will be incorporated in the class lessons.

Candidates who fail the questions on accident procedure, but pass the rest of the test, will be required to produce a first-aid certificate, to be sent in to the Examinations Office before their result is confirmed.

2 Where to Train

Formal training at a recognised establishment is necessary for most AI candidates. Students attempting the examination on a private, DIY basis are rarely successful. It should be remembered that the BHSAI is a professional qualification which demands intensive training if the required levels are to be met.

Basically, there are two ways to obtain training — candidates attend teaching centres either as students or as working pupils.

The difference is that students pay a fee for tuition (and accommodation, if applicable) for which they receive two or three sessions of tuition per day plus a lecture. They are normally exempt from some areas of yard work and usually look after only one or two horses in order to allow more time for study. Students generally work a five-day week.

Working pupils receive tuition in return for working in the yard. Arrangements vary from one establishment to another. Some centres expect a small fee for accommodation whilst others may make a nominal pocket-money allowance as well as providing training. Pupils work up to six days per week and are usually expected to look after three or four horses. Their formal tuition comprises one riding lesson and one lecture per day, for which no fee is charged.

Student tuition is relatively intensive, lasting between one and six months, depending upon previous experience. Working pupil courses are generally held over a 12-month period or, for those with very limited previous experience, may extend to two years in order to bring the pupil up to standard.

Part-time courses tailored to suit individual needs may be available at some establishments but these will normally involve the payment of student fees.

Training Establishments

It is recommended that students and working pupils train at a BHS-approved riding establishment. The Society's booklet *Where to Ride* lists all BHS-approved establishments in the UK, defining the levels to which teaching centres are equipped to train candidates.

It is an advantage to attend a centre which offers training for the BHSII or even BHSI exams. The standard of tuition and horses should be higher than otherwise and the general facilities more comprehensive. However, it is always worth checking the qualifications of the centre's chief instructor. A BHSII or above is always preferable but it should not be forgotten that there are also some very experienced AIs who achieve equally good pass rates for their students.

An increasing number of technical colleges are now offering courses leading to the BHSAI and other horse-related examinations in conjunction with general education leading to GCSE, 'A' level, secretarial or business qualifications. Most of them advertise their courses regularly in the equestrian press.

Assessment

Having chosen one, or several, possible training schools, it is advisable to arrange for assessment interviews. These will give the prospective pupil a chance to inspect the centre, its horses, facilities etc, and for the chief instructor to assess the level of riding and advise on the probable length of the training period.

Before embarking on training it is sensible for a contractual agreement to be drawn up detailing the work expected of the pupil, the tuition to be given etc.

YTS

Prospective pupils of 16–17 years of age may be able to apply to train under the Youth Training Scheme. This scheme provides a weekly payment to help with living costs while training. However, any accommodation fees required by the centre have to be paid out of this amount. YTS arrangements normally apply only to working pupils and payments can last for up to two years. Further details are available from Jobcentres or Careers Offices.

3   Horse Physiology

Classification

The following terms are used in describing horses:

General

- Stallion/Entire   uncastrated male
- Gelding   castrated male of any age
- Mare   female of any age
- Colt   male up to three years old
- Filly   female up to three years old
- Foal   horse of either sex up to one year old
- Yearling   one-year-old horse
- Mule   progeny of donkey stallion out of a horse/pony mare
- Jennet/Hinny   progeny of horse/pony stallion out of a she-ass

Colours

- Black   black pigment throughout full coat
- Brown   mixture of black/brown pigment in coat with black mane, tail and points
- Bay   variations of brown and brown/red with black mane, tail and points
- Dun   yellow or blue with black mane, tail and points
- Chestnut   yellow/gold and red/gold of various shades with mane and tail of body colour or lighter
- Grey   mixture of white/black hairs growing paler with age
- Dapple Grey   regular-sized spots of grey/white fading with age

- Flea-bitten Grey   grey or white coat flecked with darker hair
- Blue Roan   mixture of black or brown and white hairs giving a bluish tinge
- Bay or Red Roan   mixture of bay and white hairs giving a reddish tinge
- Strawberry Roan   mixture of chestnut and white hairs giving a pinkish tinge
- Palomino   golden with white mane or tail
- Appaloosa   a spotted coat: leopard spotted—dark spots on a lighter background; snowflake marking—white spots on a darker background; blanket marking—leopard spots on the rump area only
- Piebald   large, irregular patches of black and white
- Skewbald   large, irregular patches of any other colour and white
- Albino   white with pink or blue eyes due to a congenital absence of pigment

Markings

Head:
- Star   white spot on forehead
- Stripe   narrow white line down face
- Blaze   broad white line down face, including the muzzle
- Snip   white mark between nostrils
- White Face   very wide mark covering most of the face
- Mealy Muzzle   pale brown muzzle on a darker coloured animal

Limbs:
- Ermine Marks   white marks round the coronet
- Sock   a white leg up to the top of the cannon bone

Height

A horse's height is measured in hands—one hand is equal to 10 cm (4 in) and is expressed as h.h., i.e. hands high. The height is taken from the highest part of the wither to the ground when the horse is standing level. If the horse is wearing shoes, 1.25 cm (½ in) is allowed to calculate the true height. The Joint Measurement Scheme (at the BHS) issues height certificates for horses and ponies of six years and over who must be unshod at the time of measurement. They are measured by an official of the Scheme.

Breeds

There are hundreds of different breeds of horses and ponies around the world. The following is a list of the riding horses and ponies generally found in Great Britain:

Native Breeds

Breed	Origin	Height	Colours
Shetland	Shetland Isles	10.2h.h.	Any
Highland	Highlands	12.2–14.2h.h.	Shades of dun, grey, brown, black etc
Fell	W. of Pennines	13.2–14h.h.	Black, brown, bay, grey
Dale	E. of Pennines	Up to 14.2h.h.	Mainly black
Welsh Sect. A	Wales	Up to 12h.h.	Any except piebald and skewbald
Welsh Sect. B	Wales	Up to 13.2h.h.	
Welsh Sect. C	Wales	Up to 13.2h.h.	
Welsh Sect. D	Wales	14.2h.h. upwards	
New Forest	New Forest	12–14h.h.	Bay or brown predominate
Dartmoor	Dartmoor	Up to 12.2h.h.	Bay, black, brown
Exmoor	Exmoor	Up to 12.2h.h.	Bay, brown, dun with black points and mealy muzzle
Connemara	Ireland	13–14h.h.	Grey, dun, black, brown, bay

Other Breeds

Thoroughbred, Arab, Anglo-Arab (Arab cross Thoroughbred), Cleveland Bay (Yorkshire), Irish Draught (Ireland)

Warm-bloods (Hanoverians, Holsteins, Dutch etc) are in general use throughout Europe.

Types

- Hunter   usually half or three-quarters Thoroughbred. In the show ring hunters are classified in three categories:
  Lightweight capable of carrying 79 kg (12½ st);
  Middleweight capable of carrying 86 kg (13½ st);
  Heavyweight capable of carrying 92 kg (14½ st)
- Hack   quality lightweight riding-horse, usually Thoroughbred or nearly so
- Riding Horse   all-round horse for general riding
- Polo Pony   fast, Thoroughbred ponies often of Argentinian origin. Always described as a pony irrespective of height
- Cob   heavy, close-coupled, thick-set, weight-carrying horse

When describing a horse for examination purposes the following information is given:

a. Size
b. Colour
c. Sex
d. Age (at this level candidates are not expected to age the horse)
e. Markings
f. General description of type and breeding
g. Some information about the horse's abilities, competition results and participations (if known)
h. Suggestions as to the job for which the horse would be suitable
i. General observations on conformation

Conformation

First impressions are often a good indication when assessing conformation, after which a more detailed study should be made. A horse's conformation should always be related to the purpose for which he is kept. The make-up of a cob, for instance, however good of its kind, would be quite unsuitable for a horse bought with the intention of eventing.

Head — Refined in appearance with an alert expression. Eyes large, ears large and mobile, wide nostrils to permit maximum inhalation of air. Jawbones well spaced, sufficient to allow insertion of a closed fist, so that the horse is able to flex at the poll. Mouth should be neither over-shot (parrot mouth) nor under-shot. Both cause bitting and feeding problems.

Neck — As a guide to proportion, the length of the neck should be one and a half times the measurement from the poll, down the face, to the lower lip. The neck needs to be relatively long, the arched top-line being longer than the underside. It should streamline into the shoulders at the base and into the head at the top. A ewe neck, where there is pronounced muscular development in the underside, is to be avoided.

Withers — Well defined in the riding horse. In the mature horse the withers should be in line with the croup. The withers provide the attachment point for the muscles of the forehand and the back, and their position and shape largely govern the slope of the shoulder. Flat withers, loaded with muscle, cause deterioration in the action and are to be avoided in the riding horse.

Shoulders — The scapula (shoulder blade) needs to be long in relation to the humerus if the stride is to be long, low and economical. The slope of a good shoulder from the wither to its point is approximately 45 degrees in relation to the ground and this should match the angle of the pastern. The opposite condition, an upright shoulder, limits the length of the stride, calls for more effort in movement and increases the concussive effect.

Chest — Wide chests produce a round, rolling action which is not conducive to effective movement in the riding horse. Too narrow a chest causes the lower limbs to brush against each other. The ideal lies between the two extremes.

Back — The back needs to be strong. Ideally the measurement from the point of the shoulder to the last of the "false" ribs will be nearly twice that taken from the rear of the withers to the croup. Long backs are potentially weak, but a mare may be allowed a little more length here than a gelding or stallion. Very short backs are undesirable, being less able to absorb concussion whilst not being conducive to speed or comfort. Broad backs affect the action and cause saddle fitting difficulties. Faults are sway backs (dipped) or the opposite, a roach (convex) back. The loin muscles must be thick, short, powerful and broad if the full propulsive thrust of the quarters is to be realised. Space between the last rib and the angle of the haunch indicates too long a loin.

Body — The measurement of the girth is significant. The distance from the top of the wither to behind and below the elbow should equal the distance from the last point to the ground, giving the horse the appearance of being short-legged. There are eight "true" ribs attached to the vertebrae and sternum bone (sternal ribs) and ten "false" ribs attached only to the vertebrae (asternal). If the girth is deep the former are longer and flatter than the false ribs to allow the rider's thigh to lie behind the triceps muscles. The "false" ribs need to be rounded, "well-sprung" and reasonably long. They lie over the kidneys and other vital organs. If these ribs are too short the horse will "run up light" when in work, resembling a greyhound. Too much space (anything more than a hand's breadth) between the last rib and the hip bone is a serious failing and a major structural weakness. It is termed "short of a rib".

Forelegs — It should be possible to drop a vertical line from the point of the shoulder through the centre of the knee, fetlock and foot without there being any deviation of the limb from that line. The elbow should stand clear of the ribs and should not be "tied-in". The forearm needs to be long and powerfully muscled. Knees should be large, flat and an identical pair. A "calf knee" is when the limb curves inwards below the joint. "Tied in below the knee" refers to a limb in which the measurement below the knee is less than that taken lower down. Both are serious faults which can lead to tendon troubles. "Over at the knee" is when the cannon slopes back below the joint. It generally has no ill-effect on action. Cannon bones need to be

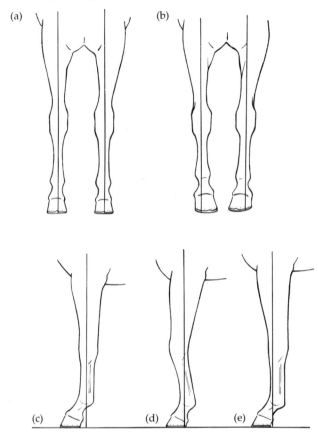

Foreleg conformation: (a) good conformation, (b) pigeon toes, (c) good conformation, (d) over at the knee, (e) back at the knee

short, strong and thick, i.e. the measurement below the knee ("bone") needs to be substantial in relation to the horse's overall weight-carrying capacity. Twenty cm (8 in) below the knee fits a horse to carry 70–80 kg (11–12 st).

Quarters—The prime requirement is that these should be powerful. Viewed from behind they should be well rounded, widening into strongly developed gaskins (second thighs). A bad fault is for the join of the thigh to occur too far up under the dock. Low-set tails and a pronounced downward slope usually accompany weak quarters.

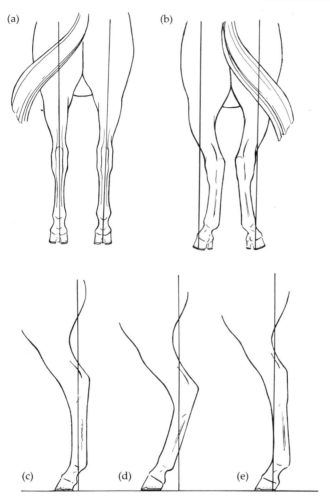

Hindleg conformation: (a) good conformation, (b) cow hocks, (c) good conformation, (d) sickle hock, (e) out behind

Hindlegs — The general rule is that a line dropped from the point of the buttock to the ground should touch the point of the hock and continue down the vertical line formed by the rear of the cannon bone. Hocks need to be low to the ground, large, well formed and an identical pair. They should not be lumpy or lymphatic. The point of the hock should be in line with the chestnut lying just above the knee of the foreleg. The second thigh will then be long and the cannon short. Faults include cow-hocks (points too close together), bowed hocks (the opposite) and "sickle" hocks which are over-bent and curved on the front surface.

Pasterns—These are part of the shock-absorbing system. If too short they are less able to cope with concussion. If over-long the horse is comfortable but may possess a potential structural weakness. Hind pasterns are always a little shorter than those in front.

Feet—The feet should be exactly matching pairs, facing directly to the front, being neither pigeon-toed (pointing inwards) nor splayed (pointing out). Small, "boxy" feet or ones notably smaller than their partners are often prone to disease. The feet should be deep and open at the heels with the soles concave rather than flat and the frog well formed and prominent.

Movement—Movement is the result of conformation and shortcomings in the horse's make-up will be reflected in the action. When the horse is trotted out it is easy to see whether the limbs are carried in a straight line or whether the feet turn in or out. The following points may be noted:

a. When each joint flexes fully it should be possible to see the sole of the foot at some time during each stride.
b. If the stifle moves outwards as the joint flexes then the hock is out of line and is being turned inwards.
c. Viewed from the side the points of the hock should rise to the same level when the joint is flexed. If one is lifted lower than the other then there may be a spavin in the hock.
d. A hind shoe showing more wear than its partner indicates imperfect joint flexion. Ideally wear on all four shoes should be equal.

Faulty Action

a. Dishing—One or both front feet are thrown outwards. It is normally only unsightly but can cause strain in the fetlock joint if excessive.

b. Plaiting—One foot is placed in front of the other, particularly in narrow-chested horses, which can lead to stumbling or falling.

c. Brushing—The legs are brushed against each other, normally in the fetlock area. This usually occurs in horses with turned-out toes.

d. Forging—The toe of the hind shoe strikes the inside of the front shoe on the same side. It is not considered to be a defect and is normally correctable.

e. Overreaching—The toe of the hind shoe catches the heel (or occasionally higher up the leg) of the foreleg on the same side.

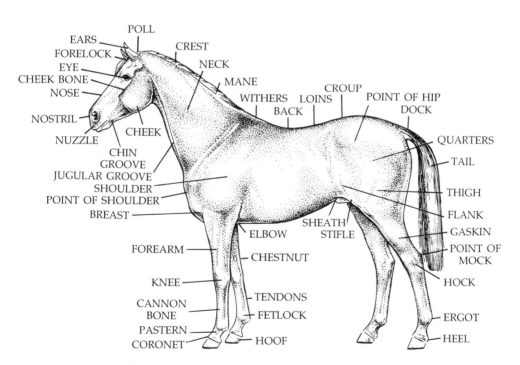

Points of the horse

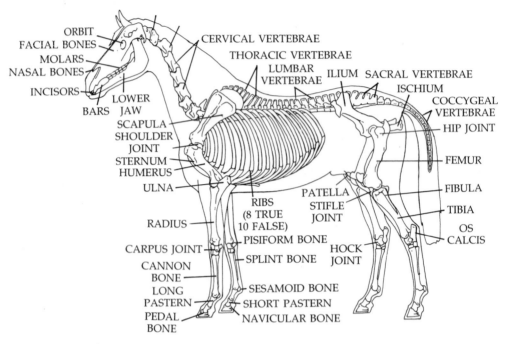

Skeletal structure of the horse

Skeletal System

The main functions of the skeleton are:

    a. To protect the vital organs.
    b. To maintain the horse's shape.
    c. To allow movement.
    d. To give points of attachment for muscles, tendons etc.

Muscular System

There are three types of muscle:

    a. Voluntary (striped) which is found in the legs, neck, quarters etc. The horse has complete control over these muscles.
    b. Involuntary (smooth) which is found in the alimentary canal, the walls of the arteries etc. The horse has no conscious control over these muscles.
    c. Cardiac which is found in the heart and contracts rhythmically.

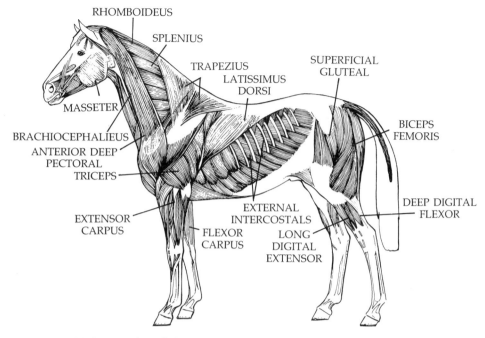

RHOMBOIDEUS
SPLENIUS
TRAPEZIUS
LATISSIMUS
DORSI
SUPERFICIAL
GLUTEAL
MASSETER
BRACHIOCEPHALIEUS
ANTERIOR DEEP
PECTORAL
TRICEPS
BICEPS
FEMORIS
EXTENSOR
CARPUS
FLEXOR
CARPUS
EXTERNAL
INTERCOSTALS
LONG
DIGITAL
EXTENSOR
DEEP DIGITAL
FLEXOR

Main muscles of the horse

When considering the anatomy of the riding horse it is the voluntary muscles which are of significance. These are divided into two groups — flexor muscles which bend the joint and extensor muscles which straighten the joint. When a horse is standing both muscles act simultaneously to stabilise the joint, thus preventing either flexion or extension.

The muscular system includes the tendons, which attach the muscles to bone, and the ligaments which hold bones together and act as support to a joint. Both are made up of hard fibres but ligaments are not as elastic as tendons. Both are liable to strain or sprain. There are four tendons in the foreleg and three in the hindleg.

The stay apparatus is a system of ligaments, tendons and muscles in the legs which support the horse, reduce concussion and prevent over-extension.

The suspensory ligament runs down the back of the cannon bone to support the fetlock and prevent it from touching the ground, and to a lesser extent it supports the tendons.

The check ligament runs from the back of the knee and stops halfway down the cannon bone where it joins the deep flexor tendon which it helps to support.

Circulatory and Lymphatic Systems

Blood circulates the body continually for the following purposes:

    a. It carries oxygen from the lungs to all parts of the body.
    b. It carries nutrients (the products of digestion) to all parts of the body.
    c. It transports carbon dioxide to the lungs for exhalation.
    d. It transports waste material to the kidneys for excretion as urine.
    e. It transports sweat to the skin.
    f. It carries hormones from the glands to all parts of the body.
    g. It helps to regulate temperature.
    h. It is a defence system against disease.

Blood consists of a straw-coloured liquid called plasma in which are suspended the following particles:

    a. Red corpuscles which carry oxygen.
    b. White corpuscles which fight infection.
    c. Platelets which are responsible for clotting blood.

The heart acts as a pump to keep the blood circulating. The heart rate of a healthy adult horse at rest is normally 36—40 beats per minute (up to 45 beats per minute in youngstock) but it can increase to over 120 beats per minute at the gallop.

Blood enters the heart from the *vena cava*, the largest vein. It passes into one of the four chambers of the heart, the right atrium, and then into another, the right ventricle. It then passes into the lungs via the *pulmonary artery* where it collects oxygen before travelling back to the heart via the *pulmonary vein*.

It then passes through the other two chambers of the heart, the left atrium and the left ventricle respectively, before leaving the heart by the *aorta*, the main artery. The blood travels around the whole body, supplying the tissues with oxygen and nutrients before returning to the heart once more.

The lymphatic system is closely related to the blood system. It consists of a fine network of vessels which join the lymphatic glands together.

Lymph, the plasma-like liquid which is conveyed around these vessels, has the following functions:

  a. To assist the blood in scavenging.
  b. To fight infection.
  c. It is responsible for maintaining the balance of intercellular fluid in the tissues.

When an infection or injury occurs, lymph travels to the area to assist the blood in fighting the infection and it is this accumulation of fluid which causes swelling.

Respiratory System

Respiration is the process by which oxygen from the air enters the blood whilst carbon dioxide is removed. It is responsible for:

  a. The introduction of oxygen into the body and the elimination of carbon dioxide.
  b. The elimination of water vapour.
  c. The regulation of body temperature.

The air is breathed in (inhalation or inspiration) through the nose and passes down the nasal passage to the *pharynx* (windpipe). A small flap called the *epiglottis* covers the top of the *oesophagus* (the passage to the stomach) to ensure that the air travels down the *pharynx* to the lungs and not into the stomach. The *larynx*, which is situated approximately one inch down the *pharynx*, is responsible for producing sound and stops impurities from passing into the lungs.

In the lungs, oxygen passes into the blood system and carbon dioxide, a waste product, is removed. The carbon dioxide passes out of the body on breathing out (exhalation or expiration).

A healthy horse at rest has a respiratory rate of 8–15 breaths per minute (i.e. 8–15 inhalations and exhalations).

Digestive System

In the natural environment the horse eats for 20–22 hours per day and sleeps for two to four hours. The stomach is small (18–27 litres/4–6 gal capacity) and digestion is a constant process, the stomach normally being kept approximately two-thirds full.

The horse feels for food with the whiskers and takes it into his mouth with the lips.

The food begins to be digested in the mouth by the saliva which makes the food four times its original weight. The horse produces 27 litres (6 gal) of saliva per day.

The food is chewed and swallowed, passing along the alimentary canal to the stomach. Because the horse is designed to eat "uphill" (i.e. grazing with the head down) the muscles which propel the food along the alimentary canal are very strong.

Food stays in the stomach for two hours where it is further digested by muscular action and gastric juices. It then passes into the small intestine (21 m/70 ft long with a capacity of 90 litres/20 gal) and then into the large intestine (113–135 litres/25–30 gal capacity). The digestive process is completed in these two channels and four-fifths of the liquid are absorbed before the waste products pass into the rectum for excretion. Liquid waste travels in the blood to the kidneys for excretion as urine and sweat.

The digestive process takes approximately 36 hours. Excess fat or carbohydrate can be stored by the body but excess protein cannot. It is removed by the lymph or is expelled via the urine and skin. Too much protein causes lymph to collect, causing swollen legs or skin rashes.

Much of the breakdown of food is done by bacteria which live in the stomachs of herbivores. This enables horses to digest materials like cellulose in grass.

All useful products of the digestive process are absorbed at various stages and pass into the blood for transportation around the body.

Horses are unable to vomit due to a very strong muscle at the entrance to the stomach. It is more often the case that the stomach will rupture before the muscle will relax.

Nervous System

The central nervous system consists of the brain and the spinal cord and from this an intricate network of nerves travels to all parts of the body.

Any stimulus (sight, sound, touch etc) provokes a nervous impulse (sensory) which travels to the central nervous system. A second impulse (motor) returns with an instruction to the muscle to react. Basically, the sensory nerves register sensation and the motor nerves produce reactionary movements by the muscle.

The autonomic systems control the involuntary muscles (e.g. the heart) and regulate the vital functions of the body.

The intercostal nerve is significant when riding as it is situated just behind the girth where the leg is applied.

Teeth and Ageing

The horse's natural lifestyle involves almost continual grazing. Because of this the teeth grow continually and are worn down by the biting and chewing of grass. This means that the teeth change gradually during the horse's life and this is the basis for ageing.

The adult horse has 40 teeth — 24 molars, 12 incisors and four tusks (male horses only). There may also be four wolf teeth. The main points to note for ageing purposes are:

One year   six new milk teeth in each jaw
Two years   complete set of milk teeth, now worn
Three years   centre two milk teeth replaced by permanent teeth
Four years   next two milk teeth replaced by permanent teeth
Five years   corner two milk teeth replaced by permanent teeth
Six years   corner incisors in wear; dental star on centre incisors
Seven years   a hook appears on the top corner incisors
Eight years   hook has disappeared; black hollow centres on teeth (infundibulum) have disappeared

After eight years ageing becomes more difficult and can only be done approximately.

At 10 years — Galvayne's groove appears at the top of the corner incisors and begins to grow downwards
At 13 years — a hook appears which is similar to that which appears at seven
At 15 years — Galvayne's groove is half-way down the teeth
At 20 years — it has reached the bottom
At 25 years — it has disappeared from the top half of the teeth

4 Horse Psychology

Instincts and Reactions

An understanding of the characteristics and instincts which govern the horse's behaviour is necessary for proper management and successful training.

Despite thousands of years of domesticity the horse retains the instincts developed in the wild state and remains essentially, even when kept alone, a gregarious, herd animal. Denied the company of other horses the domestic horse can quickly develop behavioural problems.

The herd instinct is still evident in the modern horse and although it can cause problems, it can also be used to advantage in training, such as encouraging a young horse to jump by providing other horses for him to follow, especially in the hunting field.

Where horses are kept as a group there will be a definite hierarchy amongst them. One horse will establish himself as dominant, with the others falling in a scale beneath, to the least dominating. Once established the order rarely changes. Horses will generally only threaten those nearest to them in the hierarchy, from whom they have the most reason to feel threatened themselves.

Membership of the herd provided security and leadership. The modern horse finds security in his stable and familiar surroundings which, when associated with food and comfort, can produce a "gravitational pull". For this reason it is not a good idea to site the schooling area too close to the stables for the horse may exhibit a tendency to hang towards his home.

Self-protection and self-preservation instincts in the horse are very strong, the main influencing instinct being fear. A frightened horse is equipped with facilities to bite, kick or strike out but is far more inclined to gallop away. In the stable a frightened horse will stand in a corner with his quarters facing the danger, ready to defend himself by kicking.

Horses are normally attacked by creatures leaping onto their backs and hence great care must be taken when preparing the horse for backing so that confidence in the handler can overcome his instinctive fear.

The senses of the horse and his natural, highly strung nature are part of his defence mechanism and give warning of impending danger.

The Senses

Sight

The horse's sight differs from our own. Human eyes contain both rods and cones, the combination of which enables us to have colour vision. The horse's eyes have only rods, suggesting colour blindness. However, horses can detect shades and textures quite clearly.

The equine eye does not have the ability to accommodate, that is to change focus from objects close by to objects which are far away and vice versa. The only way a horse can focus is to raise or lower his head. For this reason the horse should be allowed freedom of movement of his head and neck whilst riding across rough terrain or whilst jumping and it also explains why a horse will lower his head just before take-off in order to judge his distance from the bottom of the fence.

Because of the position of the eyes on the head horses have lateral vision and can see behind them, particularly when the head is lowered. This also forms part of the defence mechanism.

Horses do not, however, possess binocular vision and therefore they assess distance and depth less effectively than humans.

Hearing

Equine hearing is a highly developed sense and the large, mobile ears can be rotated to receive sounds from any direction and at considerable distance.

The mobility of the horse's ears is often a good indication of the horse's thought and feelings. Alert, pricked ears show an attentive, interested horse, ears which are laid flat back suggest aggressiveness or bad temper, whilst ears which are half-way between the two may indicate anxiety, confusion or simply relaxation.

Whilst not understanding actual words, horses are exceptionally responsive to the human voice and are well able to interpret the tone used.

Touch

Touch is a form of communication between horses and also between a horse and a human. Obviously, it is also involved in the riding of the horse when the leg pressure activates groups of receptor cells on the horse's sides. The horse's whiskers are used to touch and evaluate objects which he may not always be able to see, in particular the contents of the manger. For that reason their removal is sometimes controversial.

Smell

Smell is another sense which is more developed in horses than in humans and it plays an important part in the defence system. It is used as a means of recognition of other horses and of territorial regions, and is also involved in sexual play. The sense of smell is sufficiently acute to detect the "fear scent" given off by humans, which may explain how horses can detect a person who is afraid.

Taste

Taste is closely linked with smell and in the wild horses rely on their sense of taste to establish whether food is suitable. Even domesticated horses normally avoid poisonous plants, although on occasions they may be eaten inadvertently. Horses are also remarkably well able to detect the presence of wormers, medicines etc, in their feed and their lips are sufficiently sensitive to enable them to eat everything else and leave granules or powder at the bottom of the bucket.

Sixth Sense

The horse seems able to sense the moods of the rider and to reflect this in his own behaviour. He is also able to interpret and respond to very small movements, i.e. slight changes in muscular tension, in the rider.

For instance, a rider may feel that he has only to think "walk" whilst riding at trot and the horse will slow down. This probably results from an instinctive stiffening in the rider which the horse is able to detect.

Much of this apparent telepathy may be due to the heightened perception resulting from acute development of the conventional senses which are more sensitive than those of a human.

Application to Training

The horse is not possessed of a large brain and by his nature has limited powers of reason. He has, however, a long and retentive memory, although he is only able to associate cause and effect which are closely related in terms of time. Hence, punishment or reward should take place immediately if the horse is to understand which action this relates to.

Memory, reward and repetition form the basis of training and it is only by continually showing the horse what is required, correcting and rewarding over a period of time, that he will learn.

Rewards need not always be in the form of a titbit as this can lead to nipping and other undesirable behaviour. A pat and a kind word can be equally effective. Even the relaxation of the aid is, in fact, a reward to the trained horse, i.e. the legs are applied, the horse moves forward in response and the legs reward him by ceasing to act.

5   Stabled Horses

Stabling horses that are in work is the most convenient form of management. Stabling produces a controlled environment, making the tasks of feeding, exercising, grooming etc easier.

Stable Construction

The best stabling is a loose box in which the horse has freedom of movement and can lie down comfortably. A satisfactory size for a pony box would be approximately 3 × 3.5 m (10 × 12 ft), and for a hunter approximately 3.5 × 4.25 m (12 × 14 ft). Ideally, the door should be 1.2 m (4 ft) wide and 2.4 m (8 ft) high, being divided into two sections. The height of the bottom door should be 1.4 m (4½ ft) and the top 1 m (3½ ft).

Brick-built stables are warmer than wooden ones and do not present such a fire hazard, but they are also more expensive. Internal stabling is also becoming more widely used.

Erected on a level site the floor can be made of stable bricks or a non-slippery, hard-wearing substitute. Concrete is a cheap and easy material in general use but it needs to be roughened to reduce slipping. The floor should be sloped slightly to allow for drainage.

Well-ventilated boxes are essential. The top door is best kept open at all times and any window should open inwards from the top and be protected with iron bars. In order to reduce draughts stables should face away from the wind, preferably towards the south.

Kicking boards are desirable and should be fitted to all walls up to a height of approximately 1 m (3½ ft).

Light switches, preferably of the safe stable type, should be outside the stable, out of the horse's reach.

Doors need to be secured with horse-proof bolts which are easy to use. On the bottom door it is preferable to have two bolts, a hand-operated one at the top and a foot-operated, kick-over one at the bottom.

Stable Fittings

In general, the fewer fittings the better as there will be less chance of the horse injuring himself.

The following fittings are in common use:

a. Two Tie Rings — One at eye-level for short-racking and for the haynet and one at chest-level for tying the horse up. The latter should be fitted with a loop of string (ordinary, not baling) to which the horse is tied, as this will break easily in an emergency.
b. Mangers — Some older stables may have concrete or wooden mangers fitted. Other types include plastic mangers which fit into corner brackets or hook over the door.
c. Hay Racks — Now little used as they force the horse to feed at an unnatural level. Haynets are preferable.
d. Automatic Water Dispensers — These are easier than conventional buckets but have disadvantages such as difficulties in cleaning.

Stable Routine

Daily Routine

Horses are creatures of habit and thrive best on a regular daily routine. The following is based on one person taking full-time care of three fit hunters during the hunting season, but it could be adapted to suit other situations so long as a regular routine is followed.

This routine makes no provision for schooling sessions as these would not usually be applicable to hunters in work. In a competition yard it would be unusual for horses to be exercised by the ride and lead method but this is generally practised in hunting stables.

7.30am   Check yard to ensure that all is well
Check each horse for signs of illness
Straighten rugs. Water. Feed
Muck out and sweep yard
Replace night rugs with day rugs

8.45am   Breakfast for humans

9.15am   Skip out
Tidy yard and muck heap
Hay Horse 1
Quarter Horses 2 and 3

9.45am   Tack up Horses 2 and 3 and exercise (ride and lead — one and
a half hours)

11.30am Return and untack
Hay Horses 2 and 3
Skip out
Refill water buckets

11.45am Groom and strap each horse in turn

12.45pm Skip out
Water. Feed
Set fair yard

1.00pm   Lunch for humans

2.00pm   Quarter Horse 1
Tack up Horse 1 and exercise (canter work — one hour)

3.15pm   Return and untack
Skip out. Refill water buckets

3.30pm   Clean tack

4.30pm   Skip out and lay beds
Sweep and tidy yard
Replace day rugs with night rugs

5.00pm   Water. Feed
Scrub out feed buckets
Set fair yard

8.00pm   Check round
Straighten rugs
Skip out. Water
Late feed or haynet (optional)

Note: exercise is rotated so that each horse does two days of road work (one ridden and one led) of one and a half hours and one day of faster work for one hour. This is repeated for a further three days and the seventh day will be the day off.

Weekly Routine

The following are duties which need attention at least once a week:

    a. Muck heap removed if necessary
    b. Drains unclogged and cleaned
    c. Grooming kits washed and disinfected
    d. Cobwebs swept and windows cleaned
    e. Dampening down surface of the school and raking (if applicable)
    f. General yard maintenance
    g. Numnahs washed
    h. Tack taken apart and cleaned thoroughly

Yearly Routine

    a. Painting, whitewashing or creosoting of stables and ancillary buildings
    b. Major tack and rug repairs
    c. Clippers serviced and blades sharpened
    d. Fire extinguishers checked

Bedding

Bedding is used in the stable to provide warmth, to prevent jarring of the feet and to encourage the horse to stale and to lie down.

Properties of Good Bedding

    a. Easily managed
    b. Readily obtained
    c. Readily disposable

   d. Soft and dry
   e. Light in colour for a good appearance
   f. Warm
   g. Not harmful if eaten
   h. Of good quality

Types of Bedding

The following types of bedding are the most commonly used:

a. Straw — This is a drainage bedding. Wheat straw is usually the best
    as it is light with long stalks and is not usually eaten. Oat straw
    is less durable and has the added disadvantage that horses
    will eat it. Barley straw is the cheapest but it may have prickly
    awns which can irritate, although barley straw which has
    been harvested with a combine is often free from awns.
b. Shavings — This is an absorbent bedding. It is useful for horses with
    respiratory problems because it is relatively dust-free, as well
    as for persistent bed-eaters. It is warm, easier to manage and
    pleasanter to work with than straw but it is relatively expen-
    sive and disposal is less easy.
c. Sawdust — Similar to shavings but dustier. It is not in common use
    now because it is not so easily available.
d. Paper — A relatively new type of bedding which is entirely dust-free
    and therefore of benefit to horses with respiratory problems.
    It is light and pleasant to handle (although the shredded
    newspaper variety can be heavy when wet) and is managed
    in a similar way to shavings.

With all types of bedding it is usual to remove all the droppings and
soiled patches daily, the floor being cleared and swept before the bed is
shaken up and relaid. However, it is also possible to use a deep-litter
system, when droppings and soiled patches are removed but no actual
mucking out is done. The bed is topped up with fresh material daily,
the box being cleared entirely once or twice a year. Deep-litter is
labour-saving, economical and warm and encourages the horse to lie
down, but it has disadvantages. It is hard work to remove and it can
ferment, causing foot problems, if it is not carefully maintained.

Grooming

Stabled horses should be thoroughly groomed daily. Grooming is carried out for the following reasons:

a. To maintain cleanliness.
b. To maintain condition.
c. To prevent disease.
d. To improve appearance.
e. To promote circulation.
f. To get the horse used to being handled.
g. To create a relationship with the horse.
h. To have an opportunity to check for cuts and bruises.

The Grooming Kit

Body Brush—To remove dust and grease from the coat, mane and tail. Not for use on the grass-kept horse.

Dandy Brush—For removing heavier mud, especially from grass-kept horses. Its use on stabled, clipped or sensitive horses and on manes and tails is not advisable.

Metal Curry Comb—Used for cleaning the body brush and not to be used on the horse.

Rubber or Plastic Curry Comb—Useful for removing loose hair from a moulting or mud-covered horse. It is used in a circular motion.

Water Brush—Used dampened on the mane and tail and for cleaning the feet.

Sponges—One for the eyes and nostrils and one for the dock.

Hoof Pick—For removing stones and mud from the feet: it is used from the heel towards the toe.

Mane and Tail Comb—Used for untangling and pulling manes and tails.

Stable Rubber—Made of linen, it is dampened and used to give a final polish.

Wisp/Massage Pad—Used when strapping on the large muscle groups only (the neck, shoulders and quarters); it promotes circulation and muscle tone.

Sweat Scraper—Used to remove excess sweat or water.

Types of Grooming

Quartering — This is a quick removal of stable stains and obvious dust prior to exercising so that the horse is neat and tidy. The feet should also be picked out and the eyes, nostrils and dock sponged.

Set Fair — The same as quartering but this takes place in the evening.

Strapping — This is part of the main grooming session which is normally carried out after exercise when the pores of the skin are open

The following system is normally adopted:

a. Assemble the grooming kit.
b. Tie the horse up and remove rugs.
c. Pick out the feet into a skip and check the fitting and wear of the shoes.
d. Remove mud or sweat marks with a dandy brush if necessary (not with clipped or thin-skinned horses).
e. Go over the whole horse with the body brush, starting at the top of the neck on the near side. The body brush should be used in short, circular strokes in the direction of the coat and should be used firmly enough to provoke a reaction from the horse's muscles. Clean the body brush after every stroke or every few strokes. Gently groom the head with the body brush.
f. Untangle and brush out the mane and tail using the body brush, *never* the dandy brush or metal tail comb.
g. Massage with a damp wisp or a massage pad. This should be done very firmly, bringing it down hard against the horse's muscles in the direction of the coat, on the main muscles only (this is correctly described as "strapping").
h. Sponge out the eyes, nostrils and, with a separate sponge, the dock.
i. Lay the mane with a dampened water brush.
j. Oil the hooves.
k. Add a final polish with a damp stable rubber.
l. Replace rugs, bandage tail and untie the horse. (The tail bandage is removed after about half an hour so that there is no possibility of interference with the circulation.)

Clipping

Most horses grow heavy coats in the winter. If they are required to undertake hard work they then sweat excessively and lose condition. To prevent this horses in full work are clipped, usually in early October when the winter coat is established, and are then reclipped as often as is necessary, usually every three to four weeks, until the middle of January. It is not advisable to clip after this as it may interfere with the growth of the spring coat.

The main reasons for clipping are as follows:

    a. To enable the horse to work without distress.
    b. To facilitate grooming.
    c. To help maintain condition.
    d. To save labour.
    e. To prevent disease.

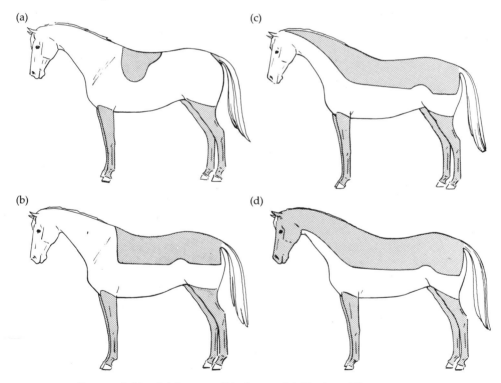

Types of clip: (a) hunter, (b) chaser, (c) blanket, (d) trace

Types of Clip

Full Clip — The whole coat is removed except for a triangle at the top of the tail.

Hunter Clip — The whole coat is removed except for the legs, the saddle patch and a triangle at the top of the tail.

Blanket Clip — The whole coat is removed except for the legs and a blanket-shaped patch covering the withers, back, loins and quarters.

Trace Clip — This clip follows the lines of the traces on a driving harness. It is similar to a blanket clip except that the hair is not removed from the upper part of the neck or from the head.

Chaser Clip — Also called a racehorse or Irish clip. This follows a line from the stifle, or from half-way up the quarters, to the poll, all the hair below that line being removed except that on the legs. The head is normally clipped but it may be left.

Sweat Clip — The barest clip possible, suitable for ponies living out who will wear a New Zealand rug. Only the hair from the underside of the neck and belly is removed.

Types of Clipping Machines

Electric Hand Clippers — These are easy to handle and are air-cooled to minimise overheating. They can be bulky when clipping tricky areas.

Electric Overhead Clippers — The far larger motor is suspended in the roof with a lead/shaft and head coming down to the hand. They are useful when there are many horses to be clipped but are more expensive and also require a permanent clipping box.

Battery-operated Clippers — These are useful and quiet but are not suitable for large clips as they need recharging regularly. They have a narrower cut and so are useful for tricky areas, especially the head, or for use on nervous or difficult horses.

Hand Clippers — These are slow and labour-intensive and are normally only used for trimming.

Small electric models, like those used on dogs, are available and are particularly useful for clipping awkward parts. They are also very quiet.

The Clipping Box

It is important to have an area which can be made available for clipping. Although a permanent clipping box is desirable, a spare loose box with most of the bedding removed will suffice. The following criteria are desirable in a permanent clipping box:

a. It has to be large enough
b. Preferably there should be a rubber-matting floor for the purposes of insulation
c. Good lighting is necessary—fluorescent strip lights are the best as artificial light is easier to clip under than sunlight
d. Sufficient power points need to be available

A clipping box can be used for grooming, washing, plaiting etc, when not being used for clipping. If a loose box is used it is important to remove all water buckets to avoid any possible contact with live current.

Method of Clipping

a. Check that the clippers are in good working order and that the blades are sharp.
b. Groom the horse thoroughly as dirt and grease will clog the clippers and blunt the blades.
c. Both the person doing the clipping and his assistant should wear suitable clothing, including rubber boots for insulation.
d. Mark out the clip with chalk or soap.
e. Switch on the clippers and allow the horse to get used to the noise. Then, holding the clippers in one hand, stroke the horse with the other so that he can feel the vibrations through you. When he is settled you can begin clipping.
f. Start clipping on an easy area, usually the shoulder. Clip against the lie of the coat using long, sweeping strokes and keep the blades flat against the horse's skin.
g. Clean and oil the clippers at regular intervals. If they show signs of overheating, switch off to allow them to cool down. Should the horse break into a sweat then stop clipping immediately.

   h. Groom the loose hairs from the horse.

   i. Rug the horse up well.

   j. Sweep up the loose hair and clean and oil the clippers. Dismantle and store the blades separately.

It is normal practice to leave the most difficult areas until last when the horse has become used to the clippers, but this is a matter for the individual. Some horses become increasingly fidgety as the work progresses and it may be better in such instances to tackle the awkward parts early on.

With a difficult horse the assistant can hold up a leg, or it may be necessary to employ a twitch rather than put up with a battle. It is possible, on the advice of a veterinary surgeon, to sedate very difficult horses.

Where a horse proves impossible to clip he should be rugged up very early (in August) to prevent a thick coat from growing. Clipping can then be avoided altogether.

Trimming

Trimming is done all year round to improve the appearance of the horse and to keep the mane thin enough for plaiting.

Mane

There are two ways of trimming the mane:

a. Pulling—This is where the underneath hairs are pulled out in order to shorten and thin the mane. It is normal practice to start at the top end of the neck, pulling just a few hairs at a time with a quick, sharp jerk.

b. Hogging—This is where the whole mane is removed with clippers. Hogging is carried out for the sake of appearance, often on horses with thick, cobby necks. Sometimes the mane is hogged for veterinary reasons (i.e. mange or sweet itch). The mane will need hogging approximately every three to four weeks depending upon the hair growth. It takes up to two years for the mane to re-grow and it may never look as good as the original mane.

Tail

The tail is normally pulled, although it is wiser to leave a full tail on horses living out to give better protection against the weather and flies. There are two ways of pulling the tail:

a. Banged Tail—The top of the tail is pulled, usually along the length of the dock, and is cut straight across the bottom so that when the horse carries the tail it is level with the hocks. Again, only a few hairs should be pulled out at a time. It is not advisable to stand directly behind the horse.
b. Switch Tail—The tail is pulled down the whole length to make a point at the bottom. This is far less common.

Legs and Whiskers

The hair around the bottom of the fetlock and round the coronary band may also be trimmed to improve the appearance, using a pair of curved scissors. Whether the whiskers should be trimmed is a debatable point as they are part of the mechanism by which the horse feels, especially for his food. However, no trimming of either kind should be carried out on horses living at grass when the fetlock hair provides natural drainage and protects the heels from mud fever.

Plaiting

Plaiting is a cosmetic exercise for special occasions. Loose plaiting of the mane may be done so as to train the mane to lie on the desired side of the neck—usually the off-side.

Mane

The traditional number of plaits for the mane is seven, with the forelock plait making eight, but a greater number are sometimes used so as to show off the horse's neck to greater advantage.

The mane is first dampened, then divided into the required number of sections. Starting at the poll, each section is plaited tightly and secured at the bottom with either a rubber band or with thread. The plait is then rolled or folded into a ball and secured with the rest of the thread or with a second band. Any stray hairs should not be cut.

Tail

A full tail may be plaited but a pulled tail cannot. The plait is begun by taking two pieces of hair, one from each side of the top of the dock, and tying or sewing them together. A third piece of hair is taken from the centre of the top of the dock and the plait is begun.

Then a little hair is picked up from each side alternately and is added to the plait as it progresses down the tail. Just before the bottom of the dock the main plait is continued to the full length of the hair but no new hair is added. This plait is then secured at the bottom, folded in half and sewn flat or left as a loop.

Care of the Hunter/Competition Horse

The Hunter

Given below is an example of a routine to be followed for a fit, clipped, stabled hunter before, during and after a hunting day.

The Day Before

- a. Give the horse normal exercise.
- b. Check that the horse is sound and that his shoes are in good condition.
- c. Check and thoroughly clean all tack.
- d. Check the location of the meet and estimate the time needed for the journey.
- e. Give an extra feed (i.e. 8pm).

Hunting Morning

- a. Feed as early as possible, at least two to three hours before setting out, otherwise try to stick to the normal routine as far as possible.
- b. Plait up after the horse has finished eating.
- c. Prepare the stable for your return.
- d. Tack up with a rug over the top of the saddle and load up. Hunters are normally transported with their tack on as even the quietest horse may be too excitable to tack up on arrival.

The Return Home

a. Keep the horse warm but give him a chance to dry off on the return to the horse box. Alternately walking and jogging is the best approach and this also applies if you are hacking home.

b. If the horse is tired, dismount and walk the last mile.

c. Do not load a hot, sweating horse as this can lead to chills.

At the Yard

a. Check the horse for cuts and remove the tack once the horse is dry.

b. Allow the horse half to three-quarters of a bucket of chilled water (cold water with the chill taken off it, but never warm) but no more.

c. Correct practice is to thatch the horse (i.e. cover the back with straw under a sheet) until he is dry, when the mud is brushed off. In some yards it may be acceptable to wash the horse in warm water, but this must not be done until the horse is cool and dry. The horse has then to be dried thoroughly before being well rugged up.

d. Feed a bran mash or gruel.

e. When the horse has finished eating brush off the mud and sweat if the horse has not been washed, but leave the detailed grooming until the following day. Check thoroughly for injury.

f. If the horse is cool and shows no signs of breaking out then put on night rugs. Give plenty of hay.

g. Approximately two hours after his return, refill water buckets and give a normal feed.

h. Check the horse regularly during the night.

i. Clean the tack that night if possible.

The Following Day

a. Follow normal stable routine.

b. Trot up to check for soundness.

c. Groom thoroughly, checking for signs of injury, thorns etc.

d. Lead out to graze or turn out for a short while.

The Competition Horse

The routine is very similar but the amount of preparation both in schooling terms and in the equipment which will be required will be greater. Check the rule book and telephone the secretary at the time stated for starting times. Allow time on arrival to tack up and work the horse in.

Transportation

Domestic horse transport is usually by road, either using a trailer or a horse box. The former is less expensive in terms of capital cost and the towing vehicle can also be used independently. When towing a speed limit of 80 km.p.h. (50 m.p.h.) has to be observed. The lighter trailers can be drawn by a car but heavier models are best drawn by a four-wheel drive vehicle, such as a Land-Rover.

Horse boxes are generally more spacious and are often considered to give a better ride. It is probably easier to load a difficult horse into a box than into a narrow trailer. Horse boxes require "plating" annually and those over 7½ tonnes require the driver to be the holder of a Heavy Goods Vehicle (HGV) licence.

Clothing for Travelling

Depending upon the weather the horse can wear either a stable rug or

Horse dressed for travelling

a light summer sheet. The addition of a sweat rug under the top rug depends upon the individual and the circumstances. Protective boots or bandages over felt pads or gamgee are necessary items, as well as a tail bandage and tail guard and a strong headcollar with a poll guard.

Loading

Horses that have been badly handled or frightened may become difficult to load but the majority will cause no trouble if a proper boxing drill has been carried out.

The first prerequisite is that the horse should have been taught to lead in hand with the handler walking at his shoulder and encouraging him forward, if necessary, by taps from a schooling whip held in the left hand and applied to the flank behind the handler's back.

The box or trailer should preferably be parked alongside a wall or gate so as to provide a wing to discourage the horse from running out. It should not be parked against the light so that the interior is dark.

Walk a circle around the box first and then make a straight approach towards the ramp, the handler looking forward and not at the horse.

A reluctant loader may be tempted with food or by loading a stable companion first to give him confidence. It may also help if the horse wears a bridle for greater control.

Two lunge lines attached to the sides of the box and crossed behind the horse just above the hocks will usually provide a successful solution but this method requires three people.

Care while Travelling

On long journeys it is advisable to stop every two to three hours to check the horse and offer water. If it is safe to do so and the horse is a good loader it may be possible to unload him and allow him to stretch his legs. A haynet can be provided during travelling but hard feed should not be given unless sufficient time is allowed for the horse to digest it before the journey is continued (i.e. at least one hour).

On very long journeys, overnight stops should be planned in advance and stabling arranged. On arrival the horse should be led out or even lunged briefly to remove any stiffness. After a long journey a horse may take several days to recover, a fact which must be borne in mind when planning the routine.

6　The Grass-kept Horse

Care of Horses at Grass

Horses and ponies may be kept at grass all year if they are not required to perform hard work, although it may be necessary to provide supplementary feed or a liberal hay ration in the winter months. The mountain and moorland breeds are often able to live out without rugs but less hardy breeds may need a New Zealand rug during bad weather.

Horses and ponies which have been clipped and are kept out will always require rugging and supplementary feed. Thoroughbred or Arab-type horses, who have only fine coats, rarely thrive if kept out all year and will normally require stabling, at least at night, during the winter months.

Daily supervision to check for injuries and general well-being is necessary but grooming should be kept to a minimum so as to retain the layer of protective grease in the coat. Removal of only the worst of the mud is all that should be required. Horses at grass should be wormed every six weeks and in summer fly repellents should be applied at least once a day.

Daily exercise is not essential but a grass-kept horse will not be as fit or capable of undertaking hard, fast work as a stabled horse. Ponies may be able to do light work on grass alone in spring and early summer when the grass is good but where horses are required to do more than the minimum amount of work adequate feeding will be required in proportion to the work done.

Field Suitability

a. Size — As a general rule approximately 6,000 sq m (1½ acres) per horse is desirable. Dividing the paddock into two parts allows for rotation of grazing, the unused part being rested and possibly fertilised.

b. Access—The field needs to be a practical distance from the yard or house with reasonable access.

c. Fencing—The best is post and rail, which is expensive. Post and plain wire may be used, preferably with the top rail of timber. The wire should be kept taut and the lowest strands should not be less than 46 cm (18 in) from the ground. Well-established hedges (other than privet, yew and laurel, which are poisonous) make good fencing but need careful maintenance. The ideal fencing would be a thick hedge with a post and rail fence inside. Electric fencing is only recommended for temporary use and horses should be shown its location. Barbed wire is not suitable.

d. Gates—These should be wide, strong and well hung, with a secure latch and should open inwards into the field.

e. Water Supply—A constant water supply is essential. Running steams are suitable if they are clean, otherwise water has to be piped or provided in some other way. Containers should be kept clean, with no sharp edges or projections.

f. Shelter—Natural shelter is provided by trees, hedges or dips in the ground. In the absence of natural shelter a field shelter should be provided. This should face away from prevailing winds, be three-sided and large enough to accommodate all the horses in the field at the same time.

g. Quality of Grazing—A well-drained piece of grazing, properly fertilised, has a reasonably high nutrient value. However, poor grazing can be regarded as useful for exercise only. The paddock should be free of foreign bodies, tins, metal, plastic etc, which may cause injury, and should be free from poisonous plants like yew, ragwort, bracken, buttercup, privet, deadly nightshade etc. The best grass mixtures are those containing meadow and red fescue and cocksfoot with some clover content. The recommended clover/grass ratio is about 30/70. Matted grasses, fog, mare's tail, sorrel etc, indicate an acid, lime-deficient soil. A soil analysis should be carried out annually and advice sought on the best fertilisers to use. Horse manure is not a suitable fertiliser because of the risk of introducing red worm to the grazing.

Field Management

Since horses are wasteful grazers it is advisable to alternate the grazing with cattle, which are less selective and will clear up the long, coarse grasses left by the horses, as well as combating red-worm infestation. Droppings should be removed from paddocks at least once a week, when water containers should also be cleaned and a check made on the fencing.

Harrowing, rolling and fertilising may be carried out annually and major fencing repairs undertaken as necessary.

The Combined System

This system is a compromise between stabling the horse fully and keeping the horse at grass and it is especially suitable for the one-horse owner who has limited time.

The horse is stabled by night and turned out during the day in winter and turned out at night and stabled during the day in summer.

This system reduces the amount of time and labour expended on exercising and mucking out etc, and may also be less costly than complete stabling.

7 Feeding

The Feed Room

The feed room should be:

    a. A suitable size for the yard
    b. Reasonably central in the yard
    c. Easily accessible by lorry for feed delivery
    d. Secure, with a good door which is kept closed and padlocked at night
    e. Vermin-proof
    f. Well lit
    g. Have a concrete floor
    h. Feed should be stored in secure hoppers and clearly marked (particularly nuts and sugar beet pellets as these can easily be confused)
    i. Feeds stored in sacks should be raised off the floor on pallets if it is not possible to have them in vermin-proof containers
    j. New feed should be placed at the back so that the old feed is used first
    k. A chart should be readily visible showing each horse's feed
    l. One person should be responsible for making up all the feeds (normally a member of staff rather than a student or working pupil)

Theory of Feeding

Food provides fuel for combustion, producing heat (energy) for maintenance, growth and repair of the body and for work. The nutrients required are as follows:

   a. Proteins — for growth and repair
   b. Carbohydrates — for heat and energy
   c. Fats — for heat, energy and warmth
   d. Fibre — to assist digestion
   e. Vitamins
   f. Minerals
   g. Water

A normal balanced diet consists of two-thirds carbohydrate, one-sixth protein and one-sixth fat.

In normal circumstances the horse should receive all the vitamins and minerals that he needs from natural feedstuffs but because of deficiencies that can be caused by intensive farming practices, additives may be necessary in some circumstances.

In the natural environment horses will graze for most of the day. On good grazing horses will do well during the growing season (April to June) if they are not in hard work. During the autumn and winter months they will, however, require supplementary feeding to maintain condition.

However, horses in work, expending more energy and using up protein etc more quickly will require a diet which corresponds to the amount and type of work done.

Feed of good quality, which is palatable and nourishing, is more economical than that of a lesser quality and results in a higher standard of performance.

Feed should be bought in regularly to ensure that it is fresh. Oats, for example, lose their goodness three weeks after crushing. Once-a-week deliveries are preferable to once a month.

Each horse's diet needs to be planned according to the individual horse's requirements and factors to be taken into account include:

a. Size — It is the weight rather than the height of the horse which is significant.
b. Age — The digestive system is at its most efficient between 8–12 years. Young horses require a protein-rich diet for growth and so do older horses, due to accelerated wastage. Very old horses require easily digested food.
c. Temperament — A fizzy horse is best fed on a less energy-giving diet such as nuts or barley, whereas a sluggish horse will benefit

from having a larger energy-giving ration, such as oats.

d. Work—A horse in hard work will need more feed than one in light work. Horses off work (i.e. due to illness) should be put onto a laxative, succulent diet, such as bran mashes.

e. Time of Year—Horses will require more feed during the winter in order to maintain body temperature.

f. Quality of Grazing—Account should be taken of the amount and quality of grass if the horse is turned out regularly.

Rules of Feeding

a. Water to be constantly available and certainly before feeding
b. Feed little and often
c. Feed the correct proportion of bulk/concentrate feed
d. Make changes in the diet gradually
e. Feed something succulent every day
f. Feed a bran mash the night before the horse's day off
g. Feed at regular times each day
h. Do not feed a hot, tired horse
i. Do not disturb a horse whilst he is eating
j. Leave one to one and a half hours after feeding before exercise, or half an hour before turning out
k. Feed a balanced diet
l. Always dampen feeds
m. No one feed should be larger than 1.8 kg (4 lb)
n. Only give boiled feeds at night as they tend to lie heavily on the stomach
o. Leave at least four hours between each feed
p. Always feed salt especially in summer or to horses in hard, fast work
q. Feed limestone flour to counteract any calcium deficiency if necessary

Types of Feed

Hay

Hay is a bulk feed which aids digestion, is relatively rich in protein and contains essential minerals.

There are three main types of hay:

a. Meadow Hay — This is taken from permanent pasture. It is soft, with thin stalks and normally a pronounced green colour. It should be clean, with a pleasant smell. New hay is too rich and should not be fed until it is three to six months old.
b. Seed Hay — This is specially seeded and two cuts are taken per year. It is harder and more nutritious than meadow hay but is more difficult to digest. It is normally only fed to horses in hard work.
c. Pre-packed Hay — Commercial hay suitable for horses with respiratory problems. It is highly nutritious so a reduction of up to 50% should be made in the concentrate ration.

Conventional Feed

Oats — The best feed for horses as they consist of two-thirds carbohydrate, one-sixth protein and one-sixth fat and are a high energy feed. Oats should be clean, hard and plump and can be fed whole, crushed or rolled. Once crushed or rolled they only retain their food value for three weeks. They are high in protein for muscle-building but deficient in calcium.
Barley — A shorter grain than oats, it can be fed rolled, cooked and flaked, boiled or micronised, but never whole. Boiled barley is a useful tempter for poor feeders or to add flesh to thin horses.
Wheat — Not a suitable feed for horses.
Bran — The by-product of the milling process, the flakes should be broad and floury. Fed damp it has a laxative effect and fed dry it has the opposite effect. In large quantities it can cause a calcium deficiency on account of the high phosphorus content. The daily bran intake should not exceed 0.9 kg (2 lb).
Maize — A very high energy feed, it can be fed cooked and flaked or micronised but is indigestible whole. It is a fattening feed and heating but it is protein-deficient.
Chaff — This is usually a mixture of 80% hay and 20% straw. It adds bulk and fibre to the feed and encourages the horse to masticate, slowing down the eating process.

Linseed — Fed as a jelly or a tea. The seed must be soaked overnight and then boiled and simmered for at least six hours until the seeds burst. Unboiled it is poisonous. It is good for putting on condition and gives a shine to the coat but it should only be fed in small quantities. It is very nutritious and high in protein and oil content.

Peas and Beans — These are very heating and should only be fed in small quantities to fit horses in hard, fast work. They are very high in protein. They must be fed split, not whole.

Molasses — A by-product of sugar. Fed in small quantities it supplies energy and tempts a poor feeder. Chaff can be treated or sprayed with molasses to improve palatability.

Sugar Beet — This must be soaked overnight and fed within 24 hours. It is a useful bulk feed and good for putting on flesh but it is not suitable for horses in hard work.

Succulent Feed — Carrots, apples, mangolds, swedes and turnips can be added to the feed and are always appreciated. They should be sliced lengthwise to prevent choking.

Cod-liver Oil — A good source of vitamins, it is useful in debility cases and also as a conditioner of the coat.

Compound Feeds

There are two types of compound feed:

    a. Nuts or Cubes — Varying constituents provide different types for general use, competition, racing, stud etc

    b. Coarse Mix — Usually either non-heating or high-energy

Compound feeds are convenient, especially for the single horse-owner, but are relatively expensive. Their form prohibits flexibility and variation but they are labour-saving and always contain the same proportions, which are devised to be a balanced diet.

Compound feeds can be fed alone or in conjunction with conventional feeds.

Water must be available at all times when feeding cubes to ensure that they can be digested. Complete cubes may replace hay for horses with respiratory problems but can lead to stable vices through boredom.

Feed Additives

Normally horses receiving a balanced diet should not need any additives. However, in certain circumstances an additive may be necessary.

Competition horses have a greater need for the full range of vitamins and minerals, but especially vitamin B12 which assists in high performance.

Stabled horses are deprived of sunlight and do not, therefore, manage to manufacture sufficient quantities of vitamin D, so a supplement, such as cod-liver oil, may be necessary.

Vitamin E is often used to aid fertility and horses with brittle feet may benefit from the addition of gelatin or biotin to the feed.

Feed Calculation

In order to calculate the amount of feed a horse requires it is useful to know his weight. This can be assessed:

a. By a weigh-bridge
b. By formula—girth squared multiplied by distance between point of shoulder and point of buttock, both measured in inches, divided by 300, equals the weight in lb.

The total amount of feed required by the horse per day is approximately 2½% of his body weight.

A horse in light work will require approximately two-thirds fibre and one-third concentrates. A horse in full work will require half fibre and half concentrates. The bulk ration must never be reduced to less than one-third of the total ration.

Feed Charts

The following is a sample feed chart for a 16 h.h. hunter during the first week of fittening work. The hunter weighs approximately 508 kg (1,120 lb) and so requires 12.6 kg (28 lb) of feed per day. This will be divided into 3.6 kg (8 lb) of concentrates and 9 kg (20 lb) of hay (meadow).

7am	0.9 kg (2 lb) nuts handful bran/chaff
After exercise	2.7 kg (6 lb) hay
12 noon	0.9 kg (2 lb) nuts handful bran/chaff
5pm	1.8 kg (4 lb) nuts handful bran/chaff carrots 6.3 kg (14 lb) hay

The following is a sample feed chart for the same horse approximately six to eight weeks later. He is now fully fit and in full work. He still requires 508 kg (28 lb) of feed per day but it is now divided into 6.3 kg (14 lb) concentrates and 6.3 kg (14 lb) hay (seed). Note that all changes in the diet must be made gradually.

7am	452 g (1 lb) oats 452 g (1 lb) nuts 226 g (½ lb) bran
After exercise	2.3 kg (5 lb) hay
12 noon	0.9 kg (2 lb) oats 452 g (1 lb) nuts 226 g (½ lb) bran handful chaff
5pm	1.3 kg (3 lb) oats 452 g (1 lb) nuts 226 g (½ lb) bran handful chaff carrots 4 kg (9 lb) hay
8pm	0.9 kg (2 lb) oats 452 g (1 lb) nuts 226 g (½ lb) bran

8 Saddlery

The tack room should be sited conveniently and should be equipped with racks etc for saddlery and vermin-proof containers for rugs, bandages etc. The medicine chest should be kept locked at all times and the tack room itself should be kept locked at night or whenever the yard is empty (i.e. lunchtime).

Saddles

The foundation on which the saddle is built is the tree, which also carries the stirrup bars. It can be made from wood laminates and fitted with steel springs along its length to give greater resilience. It is then termed a "spring-tree". Saddles made without the addition of springs are said to be made on a rigid tree. Some more modern saddles are based on moulded plastic trees.

Saddle trees are made in three width fittings, with an extra broad one for ponies, and in sizes from 14—18 in in length (i.e. from the pommel to the cantle).

Saddles are filled with a material called "flocking" which can, over a period of time, shift or flatten, changing the shape and fit of the saddle, as well as the comfort for the rider. Reflocking should take place

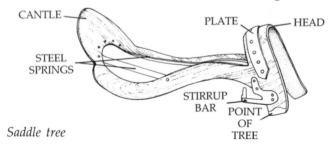

CANTLE — PLATE — HEAD
STEEL SPRINGS — STIRRUP BAR — POINT OF TREE

Saddle tree

approximately once a year to reshape and balance the saddle. However, this process will not make a saddle which does not fit a horse any more likely to fit.

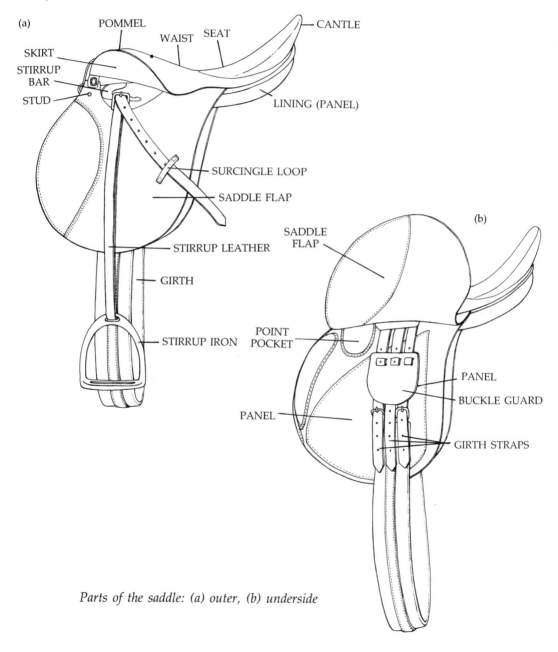

Parts of the saddle: (a) outer, (b) underside

Types of Saddle

There are three main types of saddle:

a. Dressage — A straight-cut, deep-seated saddle with the bar extended to the rear to assist the positioning of the leg. It may be fitted with long girth straps, requiring a shorter girth to remove the girth buckles from under the rider's thigh and so increase close contact with the horse.
b. Jumping — A forward-cut, flatter saddle, allowing the rider to slide the seat backwards over a fence so as to be over the horse's centre of gravity.
c. General Purpose — A saddle between these two extremes which is the most suitable for everyday purposes.

A relatively new introduction is the "synthetic saddle" which is light, cheap and easy to maintain but has a limited life expectancy.

Saddle Fitting

Always fit a saddle without a numnah or saddle cloth so that the fit of the saddle can be clearly assessed.

The rules of fitting are as follows:

a. The tree of the saddle must fit the horse's back. If the tree is too wide the pommel will press on the withers. If it is too narrow then it will pinch on either side of the withers.
b. The saddle should fit evenly on the muscles on either side of the horse's spine to ensure even distribution of the rider's weight
c. There should be a clear passage all the way along the horse's spine
d. There should be space for four fingers to be inserted between the pommel and the horse's withers without a rider in the saddle, and two fingers' width with a rider.
e. The saddle should lie flat on the horse's back
f. The saddle should be the right size and length for the horse and should also fit the rider

Newer saddles will settle more quickly onto the horse than second-hand ones. When buying a second-hand saddle always check it for the wear of the leather, the flocking and the safety of the stitching.

Saddle Accessories

Numnah — Although the saddle should fit without a numnah, extra protection for the back can be obtained by using one and this also has the advantage of keeping the panel of the saddle clean. Numnahs may be made of plastic materials, quilted cotton, sheepskin or simulated sheepskin and are available in three sizes — pony, cob and full — and in various shapes to fit different types of saddle.

Girth — Girths may be made of leather, cotton-covered foam, nylon string, tubular lampwick or webbing. They come in a variety of designs, including three-fold, Balding and Atherstone. Dressage girths are made in the Lonsdale pattern which has padding under the buckles. Girths are measured from buckle end to buckle end and come in sizes between 91–137 cm (36–54 in) in 5 cm (2 in) intervals.

Stirrup Leathers and Irons — The best stirrup leathers are made from oak-bark-tanned ox-hide or from red buffalo hide which, although it will stretch, is virtually unbreakable. Stirrup irons are normally made of stainless steel and need to be one or two sizes larger than the rider's boot to reduce the risk of the foot becoming trapped in the event of a fall.

Buckle Guards — Buckle guards are fitted to the girth straps to protect the saddle flap from being damaged by the girth buckles.

Breastplates — These are sometimes necessary on a horse whose saddle is inclined to slip backwards. The leather hunting breastplate resembles a martingale and is secured at one end to the girth between the forelegs and at the other to the saddle dees. Racing breastplates circle the chest and are kept in place by a strap over the neck.

Crupper — This is used to prevent the saddle from slipping forward, especially on ponies with little shoulder. It attaches to the dee on the cantle of the saddle and passes round the tail.

Bridles

There are five main groups:

    a. Snaffle
    b. Double or Weymouth
    c. Pelham
    d. Gag
    e. Bitless bridle

The bit may act on one or more of the following areas, depending upon the type of bit and its action:

    a. The bars of the mouth
    b. The corners of the mouth
    c. The tongue
    d. The chin groove
    e. The poll
    f. The lips
    g. The nose
    h. The roof of the mouth (less common)

The snaffle action is mainly on the tongue and the corners of the mouth, although this will vary with the position of the horse's head. On the young horse in a long outline the action is upwards against the lips. As the head approaches the vertical the bit acts increasingly across the lower jaw.

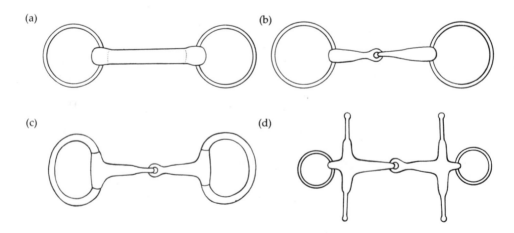

(a)   (b)

(c)   (d)

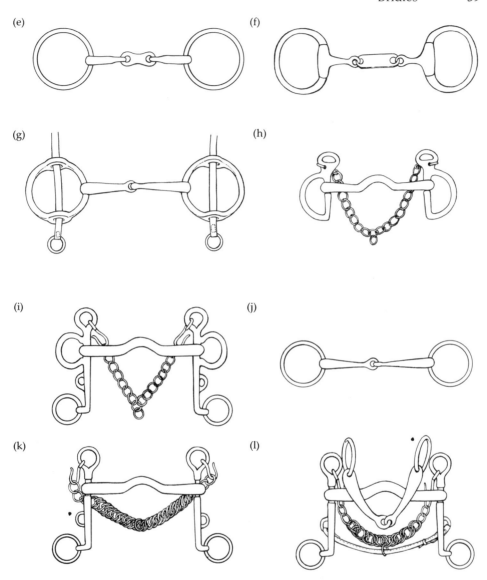

Types of bit in common use: (a) rubber or vulcanite straight bar snaffle, (b) loose-ringed snaffle, (c) eggbutt snaffle, (d) Fulmer snaffle, (e) French-link snaffle, (f) Dr. Bristol snaffle, (g) gag snaffle, (h) kimblewick, (i) pelham, (j) loose-ringed bridoon, (k) curb bit with sliding mouthpiece, (l) set of bits for the double bridle

The double bridle consists of a bridoon and a curb bit fitted with a curb chain. The bridoon acts on the corners of the mouth, rather like a snaffle, to raise the horse's head, whilst the curb acts on the bars of the mouth, the tongue, the chin groove and the poll to lower the head. The amount of poll pressure is governed by the length of the curb bit cheek-piece above the bit and curb chain pressure is governed by the length of the cheek-piece below the mouthpiece. A port in the mouthpiece accommodates the tongue and allows more direct pressure on the bars.

The pelham is a compromise between the snaffle and the double bridles, having one mouthpiece and two reins which need to be used independently if the action of the bit is to be effective. Despite theoretical problems the pelham works very well for some horses, possibly because of its indefinite action. It may be used with roundings and one rein when its action will be less precise.

The gag acts in a similar way to the ordinary snaffle but it has the added action of increased upward pressure on the corners of the mouth because the leather cheek-pieces, to which the rein is attached, pass through the centre of the bit rings and raise the bit in the horse's mouth. It should always be used with an ordinary snaffle rein in addition to the gag rein.

The bitless bridle acts mainly on the chin groove, the nose and the poll.

The basic types of snaffle bits have either jointed or mullen mouthpieces. Bit rings are either loose, which allows movement or "play" in the mouthpiece, eggbutt, which restricts movement but prevents pinching of the lips, and the cheek-piece snaffles, like the Fulmer, which give emphasis to the lateral action of the bit.

Links or spatulas incorporated into the mouthpiece reduce the nutcracker action and, with the exception of the Dr Bristol where the link is angled, are considered to be milder in their effect than single jointed snaffles.

Curb bits, which have a variety of ports allowing for varied pressure on the tongue or bars, may be either fixed or sliding-cheeked. The sliding-cheek curb allows movement of the mouthpiece but it also allows extra length to the cheek-piece and so is slightly stronger. Bridoons may be either loose-ringed, normally used with a sliding-cheek curb, or eggbutt, normally used with a fixed curb.

Nosebands

These may supplement or alter the bit action.

The most common is the cavesson, used mainly for aesthetic purposes, although it is the only noseband to allow the fitting of a standing martingale. It may be used to assist in closing the horse's mouth.

The drop noseband fastens below the bit and prevents the mouth being opened by adding pressure on the nose.

The flash noseband is a combination of the cavesson and the drop. It prevents the mouth from being opened but applies less pressure than the drop. A standing martingale may be fitted to the cavesson part.

The grakle noseband is a crossed or figure-of-eight noseband which places pressure on the centre of the nose in one spot and so is more direct in action. It applies pressure to the nose to keep the mouth closed and prevents the jaws being crossed.

Bridle Fitting

The bit should project about 0.5–1.25 cm (¼–½ in) at each side of the mouth and be sufficiently high in the mouth to wrinkle the lips slightly. The cheek adjustment should be equal on both sides. The browband should not be so short as to cause the headpiece to put pressure on the back of the ears. The throat lash needs to be loose enough to allow the insertion of four fingers so that the horse is able to flex comfortably.

The cavesson noseband should be loose enough to allow the insertion of two fingers, unless it is being used to close the mouth when it may be slightly tighter. The drop noseband should lie four fingers' width above the nostrils and should never restrict the horse's breathing.

When fitting a bridle, hold it up against the horse's head for an approximate fit and leave all the straps out of their runners and keepers for quick adjustment.

Martingales

There are two main types and they limit the upward movement of the head. The running martingale fits from the girth, through a neckstrap, and divides into two straps ending in rings through which the reins pass. Correctly adjusted, it acts on the mouth when the head is thrown above the level of control. It is necessary to fit stops to the reins to prevent the rings from interfering with the bit.

The standing martingale is similar but has a single strap from the girth which is attached to the cavesson noseband. It prevents the head from being raised by putting pressure on the nose.

Martingale Fitting

The straps of the running martingale should be within a handspan of the withers when stretched up towards them, unattached from the reins. The standing martingale should reach up into the horse's gullet when fitted.

However, the best guide is to attach the martingale with the reins held in the normal position and to ensure that the martingale comes into action at the point where control would otherwise be lost.

Lungeing Equipment

a. Bridle — This will be the horse's normal working bridle.
b. Lunge Cavesson — Fitted over the bridle but under the cheekpieces to ensure that it does not interfere with the bit. It may be made of leather, which is long-lasting but more expensive, or nylon.
c. Roller — Made of leather or jute with a number of rings for the attachment of side reins, and dees for long reins to pass through. A saddle may also be used, when the stirrups should either be removed or run up and secured.
d. Side Reins — Plain leather or nylon straps, usually with elastic or rubber ring inserts to provide some "give". They are attached to the lunge cavesson or, more commonly, to the bit rings. Their purpose is to regulate head-carriage, keep the bit still in the horse's mouth and help keep the horse straight.
e. Lunge Rein — Usually made of tubular web or nylon which is more slippery. Length varies between 6.5—9 m (21—30 ft) with a loop at one end and a swivel clip at the other.
f. Lunge Whip — A long, fibre-glass whip with a thong and lash.
g. Boots — Brushing boots should always be used on all four legs when lungeing, especially for a young horse who is less well balanced and may easily knock into himself.

Long-reining Equipment

The equipment for long-reining is similar to that for lungeing except that two lunge lines are used. Each is attached to an outer ring on the cavesson (or to the bit rings with a more experienced horse) and passes either through the stirrups on the saddle, which are run down and secured underneath the horse's girth, or through lower rings on the lungeing roller, and into the trainer's hands.

Schooling Reins

There are several designs of schooling reins, some of which may be useful in certain circumstances, but they are normally considered to be a short-cut and should not replace proper and progressive training. Their use is not recommended to inexperienced riders.

The draw rein is used to establish the position of the horse's head whilst the more sophisticated Chambon (lungeing only) and de Gogue (ridden) are concerned with the establishment of an overall outline.

Rugs, Boots and Bandages

Rugs

A good rug provides maximum warmth and fits without risk of slipping or rubbing. Rugs are made in 7.5 cm (3 in) sizes between 1.3 and 2 m (4¼ and 7 ft). They are measured from the centre of the breast along the full length. The size for an average 16 h.h. hunter would be approximately 1.8−1.9 m (6−6¼ ft).

Types of Rugs

a. Night Rug—This is made of jute or quilted nylon and polyester. It is used with or without blankets and secured either by attached surcingles, some of which cross over under the body to prevent pressure on the spine, or by a separate roller.
b. Day Rug—Normally used for travelling and at shows, it is made of wool or Melton cloth in a variety of colours and it is possible to obtain matching travelling boots and tail guard.

c. New Zealand Rug—Used for turning out a stabled horse or for a horse kept at grass. They are traditionally made of waterproof canvas with a wool lining but more recent ones may have a nylon outerside and quilted or blanket lining. They are normally secured by a surcingle and leg straps or by leg straps alone so that they stay in place when the horse rolls.

d. Summer Sheet—Used to keep stabled horses free from dust and flies in the summer. Usually made of cotton or linen material.

e. Anti-sweat Rug—This is a cotton-mesh rug like a string vest and is designed to dry off a wet or sweating horse when used under a top sheet. It can also be used as a travelling rug on warmer days.

f. Exercise Sheet—A shorter rug, about 1.4 m (4½ ft) in length, which fits under the saddle during exercise. It may be made of Melton or wool cloth or of a waterproof material.

g. Blankets—Placed under a top rug, these are used to give additional warmth. The traditional blanket is made of striped 3.5 kg (8 lb) wool cloth.

h. Surcingles and Rollers—These fit round the horse's girth to keep rugs in place. Rollers are preferable because they are padded on either side of the spine. Anti-cast rollers have an metal arch over the horse's back which prevents the horse from rolling and getting cast in the stable.

Boots

Boots are used for protection against injury either during exercise or travelling, or for support.

Types of Boots

a. Brushing Boots—Give protection to the fetlock joint and cannon bone against a blow from the opposite leg. Front boots normally have three or four straps and hind boot have five straps, although Velcro fastenings are now becoming popular.

b. Polo Boots—A heavier boot giving protection and support to the whole lower leg.

c. Fetlock Boots—Protect the joint against brushing injuries.

d. Yorkshire Boots—These also protect the fetlock but are made of rugging, doubled over and fastened around the fetlock.

e. Fetlock Ring—A rubber ring with a leather strap running through it which is fastened round the upper part of the fetlock joint, it helps to stop injury by brushing.

f. Coronet Boots—These fit around the coronary band to protect against low brushing.

g. Overreach Boots—Rubber, bell-shaped boots which prevent the horse from cutting into a front heel with a hind toe.

h. Tendon Boots—These fit round the back of the foreleg to provide support and to protect against high overreaching, especially when jumping. They may be closed or open-fronted.

i. Knee Boots—Usually made of leather and wool cloth, these have a strap which is done up tightly above the knee to prevent them from slipping down and a lower one which is fastened loosely to allow the knee to flex. They are mainly used for roadwork and travelling. Jumping knee boots do not have a lower strap, to remove the risk of it being caught up by a hind-foot.

j. Travelling Boots—These may be separate knee and hock boots, used in conjunction with travelling bandages, or all-in-one boots which cover the horse's leg from the coronary band to above the knee or hock.

k. Poultice Boots—Used purely for veterinary reasons, this is hoof-shaped and is used to help keep poultices in place.

Bandages

Bandages are used for support and protection during exercise, protection and warmth in the stable and whilst travelling or to keep dressings in place.

Types

a. Stable/Travel Bandages—Normally made of wool or stockinette and used over gamgee tissue. They are put on from just below the knee or hock to the coronary band.

b. Exercise Bandages — A narrower, elasticated bandage to give support to the tendons during exercise. Put on over pads or gamgee, they cover the cannon bone only and should not interfere with the flexion of the joints.

c. Tail Bandages — Made from stockinette or crepe they are wound round the tail to encourage the hairs to lie flat and to protect the tail during travelling.

d. Veterinary Bandages — These are usually wide, crepe bandages which are used to keep poultices and dressings in place.

Other items of horse clothing for travelling include the tail guard, fitted round the tail and attached to the surcingle or roller, and the poll guard which is fastened onto the headcollar to protect the horse's head during travelling.

Care of Saddlery

Saddlery should be cleaned daily after use. All saddlery, including accessories such as headcollars, boots, numnahs etc, should be cleaned thoroughly once a week.

Daily Care

The saddle and bridle should be cleaned whilst they are still warm as the dirt is then easier to remove. The tack does not need to be taken apart every time it is cleaned but all the straps should be removed from the runners and keepers.

Wash the bit and stirrups and then wipe the leather with a cloth or sponge dampened in warm water to remove the dirt and grease.

Dampen a bar of saddle soap and rub the soap on the leather with a dry sponge to prevent lather forming. Rub the soap in thoroughly, especially on the back, or flesh side, of the leather which is more absorbent than the grain side.

Replace straps in runners and keepers, loop the reins up through the throat lash and pass the noseband around the outside of the bridle, slipping the strap through the keeper but not the buckle. Run up the stirrups on the saddle and lay the girth over the top. A saddle cover helps to keep the saddle clean.

Weekly Care

At least once a week all saddlery should be dismantled and cleaned thoroughly, following the procedure given above. The stitching and general wear should be checked.

Storage

If it is necessary to store saddlery for any length of time (e.g. hunting saddlery during the summer) then it should be cleaned thoroughly, soaped and oiled. It should then be liberally covered with a coating of Vaseline and wrapped in a cotton material, not in plastic as this will cause the leather to sweat. It should be stored in a dry place at a moderate temperature. If it is too warm the leather will absorb moisture, causing the stitching to rot. If possible, soap the leather every so often. Winter rugs, blankets etc should be washed and put away in trunks in the spring, summer clothing being put away in the autumn. Regular checks should be made that there is no dampness or damage due to moths.

9　Fitness and Exercise

Getting a Horse Fit

The length of time required to get a horse fit depends upon:

a. The age and condition of the horse — An older horse takes longer to get fit and so does a young one being got into fit condition for the first time. A horse which has been let down completely will take longer to get fit than one which has only had a short lay-off. Hunters who are used to being brought up and let down every year will get fit more quickly.

b. The job the horse is required to do — An eventer, for example, needs to be at peak fitness for particular competitions. The type of fitness being aimed at is also important. A show-jumper needs to expend optimum energy in short bursts, while a long distance riding horse needs the stamina to work for long periods at a slower pace.

c. Size — The bigger, more common sort of horse will take longer to get fit than a better-bred horse.

d. Health of the horse — Horses with a history of past problems, e.g. leg conditions, will need to be worked more slowly and so will take longer to get fit.

Approximately eight weeks should be allowed for getting a horse fit for hunting, 12 weeks for novice eventing and 16 weeks for a three-day event.

The following is an example of a conditioning programme suitable for a hunter which has been turned out for the summer. The programme begins in the middle of August, the aim being to produce a fit horse for the end of October in time for the opening meet. The rations that are given here are taken as being those for a 16 h.h. hunter of 508 kg

(1,120 lb) bodyweight, i.e. 12.6 kg (28 lb) total feed intake daily.

Initial Preparation — The horse is brought up and is put on a small hard feed supplemented with ample meadow hay. Necessary injections or boosters should be given (tetanus/flu) and the horse is wormed and shod. The girth area can be hardened off with daily applications of salt water or surgical spirit. Pulling of the mane and tail can begin. For the first day or two the horse can be exercised in hand, thereafter for short periods at the walk under saddle.

Week 1 — Exercise working up to 45 minutes by the end of the week. Feed ration by the end of the week — 3.6 kg (8 lb) concentrates (nuts) divided into three feeds of 0.9 kg (2 lb), 0.9 kg (2 lb) and 1.8 kg (4 lb) plus a handful of bran or chaff in each feed. Also 9 kg (20 lb) of meadow hay: 2.7 kg (6 lb) in the morning and 6.3 kg (14 lb) at night.

Week 2 — Up to one hour walking. Let the horse break into trot if he wants to. Begin to introduce some trotting by the end of the week.

Week 3 — Increase trot work, build up to a total exercise of one and a quarter hours per day. Include a little hill work. Feed ration — 4.5 kg (10 lb) concentrates (half oats, half nuts), 8.2 kg (18 lb) meadow hay, all increased gradually.

Week 4 — Increase hill work and trotting. Feed ration — 5.4 kg (12 lb) concentrates, 7.25 kg (16 lb) meadow hay.

Week 5 — Begin canter work on good going for short stretches, increasing towards the end of the week. Change from meadow hay to seed hay. A major part of the concentrate ration should now be oats. Exercise one and a half to one and three-quarter hours per day.

Week 6 — Horse now on full rations, i.e. 6.3 kg (14 lb) concentrates, mainly oats, and 6.3 kg (14 lb) seed hay. Increase canter work progressively but restrict to two or three times per week.

Weeks 7 and 8 — As week 6. Some schooling over natural fences may begin. Give the horse a pipe opener (a short, sharp gallop) to clear the wind one or two days before hunting.

Note: one day per week is set aside as a rest day. Cub-hunting will be well underway in September and October and one morning a week with hounds will be beneficial.

Interval training is mainly used for event horses and basically involves several short periods of hard work (cantering), usually three, alternated with brief recovery periods (walking) by which time the horse has almost, but not quite, recovered his normal respiration and pulse rates. This is undertaken two or three times a week and interspersed with roadwork.

Exercise Versus Work

Exercise is the process of giving the horse sufficient physical activity to keep him healthy and at his present level of fitness. The best type of exercise is roadwork, usually a prolonged, slow trot.

Work is the job for which the horse is kept and includes canter and gallop work, schooling, jumping, hunting, competitions and all work which causes exertion or improvement in the state of fitness or education.

The horse's mental and physical welfare requires a sensible combination of work and exercise.

Roughing Off

Roughing off is the gradual process of letting a fully fit horse down when he is no longer required for work and is to be turned out. It normally takes two or three weeks to take the horse from complete fitness to the state where he is ready to be turned out.

Begin by reducing the number of rugs worn over the roughing off period. Cut down the concentrates and increase the hay ration, if possible changing from seed to meadow hay. The horse may be turned out for a short period each day, using a New Zealand rug if necessary.

Reduce strapping to a light brush off and stop grooming altogether two or three days before turning out in order to allow a layer of protective grease to build up in the coat.

Before turning out check the state of the grazing, worm the horse and have the shoes removed or grass tips fitted.

Choose a mild day for turning out. If the grazing is good then feed the horse before turning out so that he does not gorge himself on the grass. If the grazing is poor it is best not to feed so as to encourage the horse to graze rather than to gallop about. A horse that has been out every day during the roughing off process is likely to settle down virtually immediately.

Check the horse several times that day and early the following morning and then at least daily thereafter. Depending upon the type of horse it may be necessary to bring the horse in at night.

Lungeing

Lungeing, like riding, is an art which needs to be learned and practised if a good and effective technique is to be acquired. Novice or inexperienced handlers should only lunge under supervision and young horses will require a more experienced trainer if confidence and safety are to be assured.

Lungeing Objectives

a. Promotion of correct muscular development
b. Lateral suppling of the horse
c. Improvement of balance and refinement of the gaits
d. Encouragement of obedience, particularly in relation to the voice
e. Development of forward movement
f. Exercise when time is limited or circumstances make riding impossible, such as saddle sores or back injuries
g. Exercise of the fresh horse before riding
h. Accustoming the horse to the lunge in order to lunge with a rider to improve the rider's position
i. Training the young horse

Lungeing is demanding and periods should not exceed 30 minutes, less in the case of a young horse. In general, 20 minutes' lungeing is equivalent to one hour's ridden work.

Lungeing Method

a. Check that the tack is properly fitted.
b. Warm the horse up, without the side-reins being attached, working equally on both reins. The priorities during the warming-up period are to allow the horse to settle and to get him going freely forward. If the horse is lazy the handler needs to take positive action to encourage him to make greater effort.

Horse equipped for lungeing exercise

c. Work the horse in side-reins, equally on both reins. The side-reins should be adjusted to equal length and fitted so that there is a light contact when the horse carries his head naturally.

Lungeing Tips

a. When lungeing to the left hold the lunge rein in the left hand and the whip in the right, the slack of the lunge rein being held in either hand but normally in the same hand as the whip. Reverse the instruction when working to the right.
b. It is permissible to walk a small circle but do not move excessively.
c. Face the direction of the movement, positioning the body level with the horse's hip so that he can be driven forward.
d. Use the lunge whip behind the horse in positive sweeps towards the hocks.
e. If the horse is lazy, shorten the rein and walk a larger circle so as to be closer to the horse, and use the whip more positively.
f. If the horse goes too fast, restrain him with the voice and a gentle squeezing of the lunge rein.
g. If the horse falls inwards, point the whip at his shoulder to

encourage him to move away and then urge him forward more energetically. Do not allow the rein to go slack.

h. Keep the circle as large as the length of the rein allows. For all except the most experienced horses, cantering requires a larger circle, with the trainer walking a larger circle also.

Ride and Lead

Ride and lead is normally used to exercise more than one horse at a time when there is a shortage of staff or a large number of horses, or where a novice or child rider is to be escorted on a lead rein.

The led horse should always be on the ridden horse's left side. The led horse's reins are held in the rider's left hand and those of the ridden horse in the right hand, which may also carry the slack end of the led horse's reins.

The led horse should walk with his head at or just behind the ridden horse's shoulder. When turning round the led horse should be on the inside with the ridden horse walking around him. The ridden horse should be asked to perform a quarter of a turn on the forehand to allow room for the rider to dismount without letting go of either horse.

Horses being led should always wear a bridle. Where another rider is being escorted that rider will have the reins and the more experienced rider will have control via a lead rein attached to the left bit ring and passing through the right bit ring into the experienced rider's hand.

10 The Foot and Shoeing

Structure of the Foot

The structure of the foot is divided into two parts—the outer, non-vascular, insensitive parts and the inner, sensitive parts.

Insensitive Parts

The Wall—Made of dense horn, it carries the body weight. It should have a healthy, shiny appearance resulting from the periople, a varnish-like substance secreted from the periopic ring at the base of the coronary band. The thickness of the wall varies but it is thicker at the toe than at the heel. It takes 9–12 months to grow a whole new wall and average monthly growth rate is 0.5–1 cm (¼–⅜ in). The angle of the wall should be 45–50 degrees on the forefeet and 50–55 degrees on the hind-feet.

The Bars—A continuation of the wall which turns inwards at the heel and continues half-way along the frog. The bars allow for the expansion of the foot as it meets the ground and assist in absorbing concussion.

The Sole—The ground surface of the foot, it should be slightly concave. It supports weight round the outside edge but is not generally a weight-carrying surface. A flat sole increases concussion and is more liable to bruising and injury. An over-concave sole reduces the frog pressure.

The Frog—The triangular-shaped structure in the centre of the foot between the bars. It should be tough, pliable and rubbery so that when it touches the ground it flattens, filling the cleft and putting pressure on the digital cushion to assist the return of the blood back up the leg. The functions of the frog are to provide grip, to keep the heels apart, to act as a shock-absorber and to assist in pumping blood back up the leg.

Insensitive Laminae—Together with the sensitive laminae, these hold the pedal bone in the foot.

White Line—Made of inferior horn, this separates the sensitive and insensitive parts.

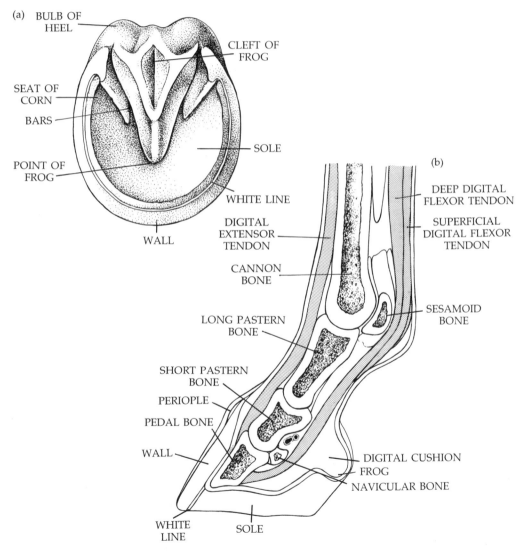

Structure of the foot: (a) underside, (b) section through lower leg

Sensitive Parts

Bones—There are two and two-thirds bones in the foot—the pedal bone, the navicular bone and two-thirds of the short pastern bone.

Sensitive Laminae—Help to hold the pedal bone in place and may break down in serious cases of laminitis.

Lateral Cartilages—Tough, slightly elastic tissues which function as shock absorbers for the sensitive foot and contain and support the digital cushion.

Digital Cushion—Similar in shape to the frog, it forces the heels apart as the foot hits the ground, dispersing the shock of impact, and hence plays an important role in reducing concussion.

Reasons for Shoeing

Shoeing is undertaken to:

    a. Prevent excessive wear of the feet

    b. Provide grip

    c. Reduce concussion

    d. Combat the effects of wet conditions which can soften the hoof

    e. Correct defects and faulty movement

    f. Assist veterinary problems

Shoeing is normally necessary every four to five weeks. Shoes should wear evenly, although the outside of the toe is usually more worn than the rest of the shoe. When it is possible to use old shoes again, due to little wear, the re-fitting is called a "remove".

Types of Shoe

The shoe has a bearing surface, next to the foot, and a ground surface. Parts of the shoe are toe, between the first nail holes on each side; heels; quarters, between the last nail hole and the heel; branches, between the toe and the heel on each side.

Hunter or riding horse shoes are made from concave fullered steel or flat iron bar. Heavy shoes cause the feet to be raised in a high action. Lighter shoes, used for riding horses, encourage a long, low stride.

Front shoes are normally fitted with toe clips which hold the shoe in place whilst it is being nailed. Hind shoes have a quarter clip on either side to prevent the shoe from shifting across the foot and to allow the toe to be bevelled to reduce the risk of overreaching.

The types of shoes in general use are:

a. Plain Stamped—The shoe has a level ground surface and is used on heavy horses or on horses undertaking a lot of roadwork, as they are very hard-wearing.

b. Three-quarter Fullered—A grooved version of the plain stamped shoe.

c. Concave Fullered—The most common. The shoe is wider on the bearing surface than the ground surface which makes the shoe lighter, improves grip and reduces the effects of suction in heavy going.

Studs

These are used to improve grip. The simplest is a calkin, formed by turning over the heel of the shoe, which is sometimes used on the outside heel on riding horses, when it is counter-balanced by a wedge on the inside.

Road studs may be fitted permanently to increase grip on the roads and may increase the life of the shoes when they have tungsten tips.

Screw-in studs are often used for competition and are fitted into prepared, threaded holes in the heels of the shoes. It is usual to have one stud in the outside heel of each hind shoe but this may cause an unbalancing of the foot so it may be preferable to use a stud in both the inside and outside heels of each hind shoe. Studs are less commonly used in the front shoes.

When not in use the holes in the shoe need to be plugged with greased cotton wool or blank "keeper" studs.

Footpads

These are normally used for veterinary purposes where the foot requires temporary protection due to injuries through bruising or as a more permanent addition to minimize the effects of excessive concussion. In bad weather they may also be used to prevent snow or ice balling in the foot.

Footpads are normally made of leather or a synthetic material and are nailed on underneath the shoe when the horse is shod. However, they may disguise problems in the sole of the foot since this may only be inspected when the horse is re-shod.

Shoeing Tools

Forging tools comprise:

    a. Anvil
    b. Fire tongs, for placing the metal in the fire
    c. Shoeing tongs, for shaping the shoe on the anvil
    d. Turning hammer, to shape the shoe
    e. Fuller, a chisel for fullering the metal
    f. Pritchel, a punch used to carry the hot shoe to the foot
    g. Stamp, to make the nail holes
    h. Punch, for making stud holes

Shoeing tools comprise:

    a. Hammer
    b. Buffer, a blade for cutting off clenches and a point for punching out broken nails
    c. Pinchers, to lift the clenches and lever off the shoe
    d. Hoof cutters, to trim the feet
    e. Drawing knife, for trimming the feet and cutting a small bed for the toe clip
    f. Toeing knife, for trimming the feet
    g. Rasp, to level the surface of the feet
    h. Tripod, a three-legged stand to support the foot whilst finishing off

Shoeing Procedure

Removing the Shoe — The clenches are knocked up with the buffer. The shoe is levered off from the heel to the toe and then backwards to avoid the toe being broken.

Preparing the Foot—The foot is trimmed with the toeing knife or hoof cutters. The bearing surface of the foot is rasped level.

Forging the Shoe—A length of metal is cut off, heated and shaped on the anvil; the shoe is heated and one side is shaped, then reheated before the other side is shaped. The nail holes are stamped and the toe clip is made. Most shoes are now made by machine.

Fitting the Shoe—Hot shoeing: the shoe is heated and placed briefly against the foot. The burn mark indicates the fit and the shoe can be altered until the fit is correct. Cold shoeing: only an approximate fit is possible so it is less preferable.

Nailing—Nails are first put in at the toe where the wall is thicker and are hammered in between the white line and the outer edge, emerging approximately one-third of the way up the hoof. Nails have two faces, the outer being straight and facing to the outside so that the nail bends away from the sensitive structures as it is driven in. The usual number of nails is seven, three on the inner branch and four on the outer.

Finishing Off—A bed is cut for the toe clip and the clenches are hammered flat. The rasp is run around the join between the hoof and the shoe.

The Well-shod Foot

Points to look for:

a. Shoe must have been made to fit the foot; the foot *must not* have been made to fit the shoe
b. Clenches in a line parallel to the coronary band
c. No rasping of the wall above the clenches
d. With ideal conformation, the angle of each pair of feet is equal and matches the angle of the pastern
e. Toe clips central in front, quarter clips behind
f. Shoe is the correct weight and suited to the horse's job
g. Shoe fits flush with the foot
h. Heels of the shoe are the correct length. Overlong heels in front can result in the shoe being pulled off by a hind foot. Too short heels reduce the bearing surface and may cause corns

i. Nails driven home flush with the shoe recess
j. The horse is sound

The Foot/Pastern Axis

The foot/pastern axis (FPA) is the relation between the angle of the pastern and the angle of the wall of the hoof. Ideally, this should also correspond to the angle of the shoulder. In a horse with good conformation this will be approximately 45—50 degrees in the forefeet with the hind feet being approximately 50—55 degrees. This ensures that the foot reaches the ground level in balance. Unbalanced feet may cause undue strain to bones, ligaments and joints and hence increase the likelihood of injury.

Corrective Shoeing

This is normally undertaken for veterinary purposes or to correct defective action. The most common types of corrective shoe are:

a. Three-quarter Shoe—A shorter heel on one side to relieve pressure on corns or capped elbows. It may also be used for horses that brush.
b. Bar Shoe—An extra strip of metal from one branch to the other provides extra frog pressure for congested heels or laminitis.
c. Rockabar Shoe—The ground surface is unlevel and the shoe rolls from back to front to assist mobility for horses with stiff joints, sidebone, ringbone or laminitis.
d. Wide Webbed Shoe—Only slightly fullered for use on horses with thin soles or driving horses.
e. Graduated Heels—These raise the heels, reducing pressure up the back of the leg for strained tendons or navicular.
f. Rolled Toes—Normally used on the hind shoes to prevent the hind foot interfering with the foreleg, but may be used on the fore shoes to make the horse move the foot away more quickly, reducing the chances of the forefoot being caught by a hind.
g. Feather-edged Shoe—The inside branch is narrower than the outside which throws the foot outwards and reduces the chances of injury through brushing.

h. Grass-tips — Used on horses turned out at grass which are not in work in order to protect the toes of the feet from splitting or breaking.

Care of the Feet

a. Maintain stable hygiene.
b. Pick out feet daily.
c. Apply hoof oil inside and out, although this is not recommended during the summer as it can soften the hoof. It is possible that the application of hoof oil to the inside of the hoof may prevent absorption of natural moisture.
d. Check the wear of shoes regularly.
e. Replace or remove shoes every four or five weeks.
f. Apply hoof grease in wet conditions.
g. If the horse is prone to thrush apply hydrogen peroxide and Stockholm tar as a preventive treatment.

11   Health

Recognition of ill-health is largely dependent upon observation of the healthy horse and is revealed in the appearance of the body, the excreta, pulse, temperature, respiration and behaviour.

Signs of Good Health

a. Alert outlook with ears pricked
b. Bright eyes
c. Membranes under eyelids, inside nostrils and inside mouth salmon-pink and moist
d. Coat flat and having a sheen
e. Skin loose and clean
f. Feed and hay has been eaten up
g. Normal amount of water consumed
h. Bed not unusually disturbed
i. Droppings normal in consistency and number
j. Urine normal (almost colourless)
k. No obvious variation in weight
l. Limbs free from any lumps or swellings
m. Horse standing evenly on all four feet (resting a hindleg is not normally a sign of illness but resting a foreleg often is)
n. No sign of sweating at rest
o. No sign of being "tucked up"
p. Horse taking strides of even length
q. Temperature normal at 100–101°F (38°C)
r. Pulse normal at 36–42 beats per minute (up to 45 beats per minute in young horses)
s. Respiration normal at 8–15 breaths per minute

Temperature, pulse and respiration may vary between individuals and normal reading should be established for future comparison. Temperature above 101–101.5°F indicates a general infection. A pulse of up to 50 beats per minute suggests that the horse is in pain. Respiration above normal is indicative of pain and an increase in temperature.

Recognising Lameness

The following procedure may be adopted:

    a. Watch to see if the horse is moving about the stable or standing unusually still and note whether he is resting or pointing a limb.

    b. With an assistant holding the horse, examine the limbs for any sign of pain, heat and/or swelling.

    c. Have the horse trotted up on a flat, hard surface, after removing rugs etc. Have the horse walked away and back in a straight line and then repeat at trot. The assistant should lead the horse at walk and trot on a loose rein to give the horse freedom of movement. Lameness in a hindlimb is normally apparent as the horse is walked or trotted away, the hip of the affected limb being carried higher than the other. Lameness in a forelimb can be detected in the movement of the horse's head, which will nod noticeably as the sound leg comes to the ground. If the horse is lame behind then often there will be nodding as the unsound leg comes to the ground. Lameness is more easily recognisable at trot because of the diagonal nature of the gait.

"Bridle lameness" is when the horse nods when trotted up in a bridle but without any unlevelness in the stride. This may indicate a bitting problem or soreness in the mouth since it will not usually occur when the horse is trotted out in a headcollar.

Lameness is more obvious on a circle. Turning a horse in tight circles in both directions will often show up lameness in the forelegs, though less so in a hindleg.

A hindleg may be held up for a short while so that all the joints are well flexed. The leg is then put down and the horse trotted away immediately. This is called a spavin test and most horses will trot away unlevel for a few strides. Those with an unsoundness, however, will be very lame.

A similar test, called a flexion test, may be carried out on most joints, such as the knee or fetlock, but should be carried out by an expert since the results may sometimes be misleading.

Once the affected limb has been established, the leg should be examined for signs of pain, heat or swelling. If the horse is very lame then the site of the injury will usually be either low down in the foot, which is common, or high up, such as the shoulder, which is much less common. If the source of the lameness is not obvious then the underside of the foot should be examined for signs of injury or bruising. If the horse has been shod recently (less than a week) then the cause may be a nail bind.

Bilateral lameness is when the horse is lame in both legs, usually both forelegs. It is typified by short, pottery strides which may suggest such diseases as laminitis or navicular.

If the horse is intermittently lame and the performance of the horse is affected, it can be an indication of changes in the substance of the bone and suggests a progressive, possibly more serious disease like navicular, sidebone, ringbone, pedal osteitis or, in older horses, an arthritic condition. Intermittent bilateral lameness may also indicate this type of problem.

If lameness is persistent or severe then a veterinary surgeon should be called but minor ailments may be dealt with in the yard.

Nursing the Sick Horse

The following should be carried out in conjunction with veterinary instructions:

    a. Watch the patient constantly.
    b. Take temperature, pulse and respiration regularly and keep a record of them.
    c. Provide a good, deep, clean bed.
    d. Keep the horse warm with lightweight rugs.
    e. Add glucose to the water to provide energy.
    f. Feed palatable, easily digested, laxative foods.
    g. Feed linseed tea if the horse is too ill to eat normally.

h. Ensure good, draught-free ventilation.
i. Groom only lightly but sponge out the eyes, nostrils and dock regularly.
j. Pick out the feet regularly.
k. Reapply dressings and poultices twice daily or on veterinary advice.
l. Check that tetanus vaccinations are up to date.
m. Isolate if necessary.

Taking Temperature, Pulse and Respiration

Temperature

a. Shake the thermometer so that the mercury is below 100°F (37.4°C).
b. Apply Vaseline to the bulb of the thermometer.
c. Insert three-quarters of the thermometer into the rectum, holding on to it firmly so that it cannot be drawn in by contraction of the muscles.
d. Remove after 30–60 seconds and read.
e. Wash the thermometer in cold water and disinfect.

Pulse

a. Place the fingers against one of the three pulse points: under the top of the lower jaw, on the horse's cheek just above and behind the eye, or on the inside of the foreleg behind the elbow.
b. Count the number of beats in 20 seconds with a stop-watch or similar, multiplying by three to obtain the pulse rate.

Respiration

a. Stand behind the horse and watch the flanks.
b. Count the number of times that the flanks rise and fall in one minute. Each rise and fall is counted as one breath.

Types of Treatment

Poulticing

Poulticing is used to:

    a. Reduce inflammation
    b. Cleanse wounds
    c. Draw out infection
    d. Reduce bruising

There are a number of good, commercial poultices which should be applied according to the instructions given, such as Animalintex or kaolin.

Bran and Epsom salts poultices are useful for foot injuries. A bran mash is mixed with a handful of Epsom salts and placed in a plastic bag. The heels of the foot are greased and the foot placed in the bag, which is secured round the fetlock. A special poultice boot or a large piece of sacking will help keep the poultice in place and will prevent the horse from eating it.

Poultices should be covered with plastic in order to keep them hot for as long as possible and to prevent them from drawing moisture from the surrounding air rather than from the injury.

Hot Tubbing

This is used for injuries and wounds to the lower limb or foot. A strong bucket is half-filled with warm water and a handful of Epsom or ordinary salt added. The heels of the foot are greased and the foot is placed in the bucket. The foot should remain immersed for about 20 minutes and more warm water should be added as required.

Hot Fomentation

This is similar to hot tubbing but is used for areas where a poultice cannot be applied, such as the hock. It is used to reduce swelling and the treatment needs to be continued for at least 20 minutes.

Add some Epsom salts to a bucket of moderately hot water and soak two pieces of thick material, such as towelling or blanket, in it. One is removed, squeezed out and applied to the area, being held there until the cloth has lost its heat. The process is repeated with the second cloth whilst the first is heated again in the water, and so on.

Cold Hosing

This is the process of trickling a gentle but continuous stream of cold water on and around a wound or swelling. It needs to be carried out for about 20 minutes several times a day. It reduces swelling and helps in cleansing wounds. The heels of the foot should be greased before and after cold hosing and the water should be gently played on the hoof first, slowly moving up the leg until the affected part is reached, to allow the horse to get used to the cold water.

The best results for the reduction of pain, heat and swelling are obtained by alternating hot and cold treatment two or three times per day. For example, the affected area can be cold hosed for 20 minutes, after which a poultice is applied for 12 hours before hosing is carried out again and a new poultice applied. The heat from the poultice and hot fomentation encourages blood and lymph to the area which speeds up healing, whilst the cold hosing encourages the blood and lymph away from the area to reduce swelling.

Administration of Medicines

Medicines should normally only be administered under veterinary advice and supervision, with the exception of routine treatments such as worming powders or pastes and external wound treatments.

Oral Medicines

These include worming powders, some antibiotics and painkillers, vitamin and mineral supplements, drenches etc. Treatments given orally may be added to the feed or to the water or given by oral syringe, as in the case of worming pastes. For a horse which is off his feed soluble medicines may be dissolved in water and given by oral syringe.

Cough electuaries and similar medications may be applied by smearing them on the back of the tongue. Powder medications may also be applied in this way if they are first mixed with black treacle or similar to form a paste. Pills may be administered by "balling", i.e. rolling them up inside tempting titbits.

When administering medicines in the feed it is advisable for the feed to be smaller than usual so as to ensure that the medicine is eaten. The feed can be made more attractive by the addition of carrots, apples, boiled barley, linseed, molasses etc.

The use of drenches, once common, is now rather controversial and they should only be given upon veterinary advice. Drenching is usually carried out for colic, for which there are a number of "colic drinks".

Stomach Tubing

Stomach tubing is the alternative to drenching, the liquid being passed directly into the stomach via a tube which is passed up the horse's nostril and along the oesophagus into the stomach. Care must be taken not to allow the tube to pass along the trachea and into the lungs. The stomach tube is preferable because it removes the possibility of the horse choking if a drench is inexpertly administered. Stomach tubing should only be carried out by a veterinary surgeon.

Injections

Injections may be intramuscular (into the muscle), intravenous (into a vein), subcutaneous (under the skin) or the more specialist intra-articular injection (into a joint). Generally, injections given straight into the vein are the quickest acting and injections given subcutaneously are the slowest.

Drugs given by injection include painkillers, antibiotics, anti-inflammatory drugs, muscle relaxants, sedatives, vitamins such as B12 and local anaesthetics (nerve blocks). They are normally given in the neck on alternate sides, but may also be given in the hindquarters, the back of the thigh or in a particular area depending upon the site of the problem.

Enema

An enema is given into the rectum to assist in removing a blockage or as a treatment for dehydration. Enemas in common use are liquid paraffin or warm, soapy water.

Inhalation

In the treatment of respiratory conditions camphor or eucalyptus oil can be added to a bucket of boiling water and the horse's head held over the bucket for 15–20 minutes.

External Treatments

These include drugs, medicines or powders applied to the horse's skin such as wound powders, antibiotic sprays, poultices, liniments, creams and astringents.

Isolation Procedure

When a horse has a contagious (spread by contact) or infectious (spread by air or water) disease it needs to be isolated to reduce or eliminate the chances of the disease spreading to other horses. Diseases that require isolation include strangles, equine influenza and ringworm.

The following procedure should be adopted:

- a. Isolate the horse by taking it as far away as possible from other horses whilst remaining within sight and sound of them if possible.
- b. Post a notice prohibiting entry if the yard is visited by outsiders.
- c. Disinfect the horse's original box and burn all bedding.
- d. Use a separate grooming kit, feeding bowls, buckets etc.
- e. Do not go from the infected horse to a healthy one. Either have one person handling the infected horse (preferable) or ensure that the infected horse is the last to be attended to.
- f. If possible use a separate set of protective clothing when dealing with the infected horse.
- g. Wash boots in disinfectant to prevent infection being carried out of the yard.
- h. Wash hands and arms in disinfectant after dealing with the infected horse.
- i. Bedding materials, dressings, uneaten food etc, should be removed and burned.

In cases where diseases are notifiable the local Ministry of Agriculture will be informed by the veterinary surgeon.

Worming

All horses are hosts to worms and unless regular worming programmes are implemented serious and lasting internal damage can result.

The common worms are:

a. Red Worm (strongyles) — These are the most dangerous. They are small (0.5—5.5 cm/¼—1½ in) and difficult to see. They live in the lining of the bowel, destroying its function. They may also invade the walls of the blood vessels and can lead to blockages of the vessels themselves. They are debilitating in the extreme and if untreated can be fatal.

b. White Worms (ascarids) — These are white or yellowish in colour, large (0.5 cm/¼ in in diameter and up to 30 cm/1 ft long) and if too numerous can cause intermittent colic and loss of condition.

c. Seat or Whip Worm (oxyuris) — These live in the large intestine and eggs are laid around the horse's dock where they can be seen as cream-coloured, waxy masses. They can cause intense itching, giving rise to tail rubbing, and their presence is usually accompanied by a discharge around the anus.

Worm infestation is prevented by:

a. Regular worming with one of the proprietary brands every six weeks.

b. Changing the wormer at intervals to prevent the worms from acquiring immunity.

c. Immediate worming of all new arrivals to the yard.

d. Stabling horses for 24 hours after worming so that the expelled worms will not contaminate pasture.

e. Picking up droppings daily from paddocks.

f. Regular harrowing of pasture, rotation of grazing and the alternating of horses with cattle.

The Medicine Cabinet

The main constituents of the medicine cabinet are:

a. Thermometer

  b. Round-ended scissors
  c. Safety-pins
  d. Surgical tape
  e. Cotton wool and gamgee
  f. Veterinary bandages
  g. Vaseline
  h. Zinc and castor-oil cream
  i. Antibiotic (wound) powder
  j. Gauze
  k. Kaolin poultice
  l. Animalintex poultice
  m. Antiseptic cream
  n. Epsom salts
  o. Witch-hazel
  p. Stockholm tar
  q. Vapour rub
  r. Disinfectant
  s. Fly repellant
  t. Antiseptic Teramycin spray
  u. Louse powder
  v. Cooling lotion
  w. Ice packs

The veterinary surgeon's telephone number should be displayed prominently close to the cabinet and the cabinet itself should be kept locked.

Minor Ailment Questions

The following are a few sample questions, indicating the type of questions that may arise on the minor ailments paper:

  a. List six ailments for which you might use cold hosing and give details of two. What could be a side-effect of hosing and how would you prevent it?
  b. What is an overreach and how would you treat it?
  c. List 12 items you would wish to have in a medicine cabinet in order of importance, with the most important first.

d. Name three parasites of the horse and give details on the causes, treatment and prevention of one of them.

e. List ten signs of good health in the horse.

f. How would you take temperature, pulse and respiration and what results would you expect to find in a healthy horse at rest?

g. Your horse has become lame several days after he was last shod. Give one possible reason for the lameness and explain what treatment you would give.

h. Your horse has a simple cough which your veterinary surgeon says is not serious. What treatment would you give and what variations would you make from normal feeding and care?

i. Name the four types of common wounds and describe how you would deal with each.

j. Explain isolation procedure and name three illnesses which might require it.

k. You have been out riding for 20 minutes when your horse begins to stiffen up in the hindlegs and seems unwilling to continue. What could be the cause and what would you do (i) immediately, (ii) over the following few days and (iii) to prevent recurrence?

12 Common Ailments

Circulatory Disorders

Anaemia

Anaemia is a deficiency of haemoglobin or red blood corpuscles. It can be caused by a chemical imbalance as a result of a deficiency of vitamin B12, folic acid or iron, for example, or by an infection, worms or lice attacking the blood content. The membranes become abnormally pale and there is a noticeable loss of energy, sometimes accompanied by a loss of weight.

Azoturia

Azoturia is also known as "Monday morning disease" because it sometimes occurs after a rest period. It is caused by a build-up of lactic acid in the muscles of the loins and hindquarters due to the circulatory system being unable to remove the products of metabolism and may be more pronounced in particular horses. It usually occurs about 10–20 minutes after the onset of exercise. The muscles of the hindquarters become hard, tense and painful to the touch and the movement of the hindlegs becomes stiff and restricted. The horse is reluctant to move, is in obvious pain and distress and may even begin to stagger.

The rider should dismount immediately and keep the horse's loins warm with a coat or rug. The horse should be taken back to the stable as quickly as possible and with the minimum expenditure of effort. It may, therefore, be necessary to summon a horsebox.

Veterinary assistance is necessary. Until it is available the horse has to be kept warm. A bran and Epsom salts mash can be offered and the horse should be encouraged to stale which will bring some relief from the pain. The urine may be a dark red or brown colour and will smell of violets.

The horse will need to be rested and the return to work will have to be gradual. Vitamin E and selenium additives have proved a useful treatment.

This ailment is prone to recurrence and should be prevented by ensuring regular exercise and a sensible diet, which must be reduced in the event of exercise being restricted.

Lymphangitis

This ailment also belongs to the "Monday morning" group. The cause is usually connected with over-feeding combined with insufficient exercise. The result is a breakdown in the waste clearance system and the circulation is unable to remove lymph from the limbs. One or both of the hindlimbs become swollen and in severe cases the horse may be very lame.

Lymphangitis can also occur from an infected cut, the infection spreading through the lymphatic system and reducing the circulation. In this case the horse will be in obvious pain and distress and will require veterinary attention. General treatment is concerned with regulating the diet, exercising where possible and cold hosing to reduce the swelling. As with azoturia, horses that have experienced lymphangitis are susceptible to recurrence.

Digestive Disorders

Colic

Colic is an abdominal pain to which horses are susceptible due to their particular stomach structure. It can be caused by sudden changes in diet, a feed which is too large, bad food etc.

The ailment is usually associated with the stabled horse but can also occur in the horse at grass, when it is more dangerous owing to the risk of it going unnoticed.

Colic can be impacted, which is caused by a simple blockage; flatulent, caused by excessive gases pressing on the gut wall; sand colic, the result of a build-up of sand in the stomach, if the paddock has a sandy-bottomed river from which the horse drinks; or spasmodic, which takes the form of intermittent spasms and is the most common.

Symptoms are general uneasiness, kicking or looking at the flanks, pawing, getting up and down and attempting to stale. There will usually be a rise in temperature and pulse, with patchy sweating and in severe cases the horse may thrash about or kick out.

The horse should be given a deep bed, kept warm and offered a small bran mash. The horse can be walked about gently without being taken too far away from his box. Where colic is severe or lasts for more than half an hour veterinary attention should be sought so that pain-killers and other drugs may be administered.

Constipation

This is caused by dietary problems and can usually be dealt with by giving laxative feeds and, where necessary, an enema.

Diarrhoea

Diarrhoea may be caused by dietary problems but it can also result from an infection (often associated with a heavy worm infestation) which is more serious and will require expert attention. Water and minerals may be lost in large quantities, leading to dehydration so electrolytes may be necessary.

Lampas

Lampas is a swelling of the mucous membrane covering the hard palate behind the incisor teeth of the upper jaw. It is most commonly seen in young horses during teething but may be caused by injuries or sharp teeth in older horses. It normally resolves itself if the cause is removed but Epsom salts added to the drinking water can also help.

Quidding

Quidding is the term used when the horse chews his food and then drops it out of his mouth without swallowing. It may be due to sharp teeth, lampas, a mouth injury or a paralysis of the swallowing mechanism. The treatment is to remove the cause and to provide soft feed if there is soreness in the mouth.

Respiratory Disorders

Equine Influenza

Influenza is a highly contagious/infectious, viral infection of the respiratory tract. The virus enters through the nose and attacks the trachea and bronchioles. The incubation period is three to four days after which the main symptoms are a cough, a nasal discharge and a raised temperature.

The horse should be isolated and the infection has to take its normal course. A period of six weeks' rest is not excessive.

'Flu vaccine is now widely available and vaccination, which is recommended, is compulsory for racehorses and many competition horses.

Strangles

Strangles is an infectious disease which usually affects young horses. It can be passed on by contact with an infected animal, from infected premises or from infected equipment.

The symptoms appear four to ten days later. Affected horses have a high temperature, a thick, yellow nasal discharge and enlarged glands under the jaw. The glands may form abscesses which burst, releasing large quantities of pus. There may also be a cough.

Veterinary attention is necessary and the horse should be isolated. Hot fomentation can be applied in order to speed up bursting of the abscesses. The horse may lose condition rapidly and have difficulty eating, in which case linseed tea or gruel may be fed.

A long period of recuperation is necessary since if the horse is worked too soon it can lead to permanent damage, resulting in whistling or roaring.

Strangles abscesses may develop in other parts of the body which is the more serious disease of "bastard" strangles. This usually responds well to antibiotics but in serious cases can prove fatal.

Colds

A cold is a mild infection of the respiratory tract similar to that suffered by humans. The cause may come from lack of fresh air, a change of environment (i.e. the horse coming up from grass), exposure or an infection.

There will normally be a nasal discharge, a slight rise in temperature and a loss of appetite and there may also be a cough.

The horse should be rested and may need to be isolated. He should be kept warm but allowed plenty of fresh air. Eucalyptus inhalation can be helpful.

Coughs

A cough is caused by an irritation in the lining of the larynx. There are three main types — those connected with a cold, those caused by a virus and those related to an allergy.

The cough may be a dry, reflex cough, the type normally seen with a dust allergy, or a thick, wet cough, which is more likely to be caused by a cold or virus.

If the cough persists then a veterinary surgeon should be consulted but in most cases the horse's hay should be steamed or soaked, an electuary given, the feeds dampened and a dust-free bedding used. The horse has to be kept warm but must get as much fresh air as possible.

Coughing horses should not be worked or else permanent damage may be done to the lungs.

Epistaxis

Epistaxis is the name given to a nosebleed which may occur during work or at rest. The cause may be an infection, inflammation, a calcium deficiency in the blood or an increased blood flow during exercise. Where bleeding occurs from one nostril the origin is likely to be in the nasal passage and is not serious. Where the bleeding occurs from both nostrils the cause is more likely to be internal, possibly from a hae-morrhage, which may result in the loss of very large quantities of blood and may be fatal.

Whistling and Roaring

These are noises made by the horse on inhalation which may be more noticeable in excitement, collection or at the faster gaits. They are caused by a paralysis of the main nerves on the left side of the larynx which causes a permanently restricted air passage.

Roaring is an exaggerated form of whistling and hence more serious. Whistling and roaring can be brought about as an after-effect of strangles, pneumonia, laryngitis, influenza or bronchitis, as a result of sudden or excessive exertion or as an inherited defect.

If the condition causes distress or results in poor performance the horse may benefit from the Hobday operation being performed in which the larynx is removed (which also removes the horse's voice), or one of the more modern techniques available.

High blowing is a noise made by the horse on exhalation and is usually the result of exertion or excitement and not an indication of any ailment.

COPD (Broken Wind)

Chronic obstructive pulmonary disease is an allergic condition caused by dust, fungal spores etc. It will be aggravated by poor general management.

The horse makes an extra effort on breathing out and seems to breathe out twice ("heaves") and coughs when under exertion. Treatment entails removal of all sources of dust, soaking or steaming of hay and the administration of a bronchodilator in powder form.

Skin Disease and Parasites

Ringworm

Ringworm is a highly contagious skin disease caused by a fungus which also affects humans. It causes distinctive circular patches of raised hair about the size of a ten-pence piece, usually first appearing on the neck and then spreading to other parts of the body. It may also appear as irregular patches on the back or face where the infection has been rubbed into the skin by saddlery. It may be contracted from other horses, cattle or humans.

Horses should be isolated, strict disinfection routines carried out and veterinary advice sought. Treatment is normally with a fungicidal wash and a course of fulcin.

Sweet Itch

Sweet itch is an allergic reaction to grass and midges in the spring and autumn and normally affects the mane and tail. Sunlight and lush grazing appear to aggravate the condition. The horse will rub the areas incessantly until they are raw and there may also be a yellow discharge.

Treatment is concerned with stabling the horse whilst the midges are most active, often in the morning and evening. Anti-inflammatory drugs can help to alleviate the symptoms.

Urticaria

Urticaria is more commonly known as nettle rash or "hives". Small lumps appear on the skin of the neck, flanks and quarters and may appear and disappear without warning. It is usually caused by something that the horse has eaten or by a sudden change in diet.

Treatment is to give a bran and Epsom salts mash and the veterinary surgeon may prescribe a course of anti-histamine.

Mud Fever

This is a mud-derived skin irritation affecting the legs. A soothing ointment, such as udder cream or zinc and castor-oil cream, may be helpful but in severe cases where the legs are hot and swollen the horse will need to be rested on a laxative diet and veterinary attention sought. Certain soils and areas of the country are more prone to cause the disease than others and prevention, by ensuring that mud is quickly washed off and the horse thoroughly dried, is preferable.

Cracked Heels

This is very similar to mud fever in cause and prevention but it affects the heels and usually takes the form of open cracks which can make the horse very lame. Treatment is similar to that for mud fever. Prevention involves cleaning and drying the legs and leaving the fetlock hair unclipped in order to provide protection. It is also sensible to grease the heels before riding or turning out in wet or muddy conditions.

Lice

Lice are the most common skin parasites on horses and they are generally found on horses at grass during the first two months of the year.

There are two types of lice, those which are blood-sucking and are found at the base of the mane and tail, and those which bite and are found on the lower parts of the body. They are more likely to attack horses in poor condition and will make the horse itch so that he rubs constantly, leaving bare patches of skin. The blood-sucking lice also make the horse lose condition and may cause anaemia. Treatment involves a liberal application of louse powder.

Warbles

The warble fly lays eggs on the horse during the summer and the larvae work their way into the skin of the horse's back and sides where they lie dormant. In the spring they appear as hard lumps under the skin. A poultice may be applied in order to encourage the lump to burst, particularly if the lump is in the saddle area, but warbles are usually best left alone as they will leave the host naturally.

Nervous Disorders

Tetanus

Tetanus is caused by a bacterium which lives in the soil and enters the body through wounds or scratches. It is a serious disease which can affect both horses and humans and is sometimes fatal. The symptoms are a high temperature, extreme distress, a severe paralysis of the limbs and eventually a paralysis of the jaw.

Prevention of tetanus by the use of regular vaccinations is recommended both for horses and for the humans who work with them.

Grass Sickness

This is a disease which produces changes in the nervous system and, although the cause is uncertain, it may be due to stress, particularly related to a change of environment, as it is seen most frequently in young, pregnant mares who have travelled to a new premises for foaling.

It only affects full or partly grass-kept horses, mainly between May and July, particularly in dry weather. There will be sweating, increased pulse and temperature and muscle tremors. There may be diarrhoea initially but the horse quickly becomes constipated. The severity ranges from death occurring in two or three days to a gradual deterioration over several weeks or months. There is little treatment at present.

Stringhalt

This is a nervous disorder where one or both hindlegs are snatched up much higher than normal, the horse almost kicking into itself. The cause is uncertain but may be related to damage of the lateral digital extensor tendon or to the nerve supplying it. Surgical removal of part of the tendon may improve the condition although some horses continue to work without treatment. However, the condition does sometimes deteriorate.

Diseases Causing Lameness

Laminitis

Laminitis, also called founder or fever of the feet, occurs when the sensitive laminae become inflamed and gorged with blood. The condition is usually caused by excessive intakes of carbohydrate associated with over-lush grazing or too rich a diet. However, it is a fallacy that laminitis only affects fat horses since thin animals may be affected due to a particular quality of the grazing at certain times of the year.

Laminitis normally occurs in the forefeet, which will be hot and painful as the laminae do not have room to swell inside the hoof. The horse will be generally unwell and may adopt the typical laminitic stance with the forefeet thrust forward so that the weight is carried on the heels.

Treatment involves cold hosing the feet to reduce the amount of blood in the foot and enforced exercise, such as leading in hand, to improve the circulation. A laxative, succulent diet should be given and only limited grazing permitted. The veterinary surgeon may prescribe anti-inflammatory drugs such as phenylbutazone.

Navicular

Navicular disease occurs because of decay in parts of the navicular bone and is usually confined to one or both forefeet. The navicular bone suffers structural changes, thought to be caused by a reduction in the blood supply to the foot, which causes the bone to become roughened so that the deep flexor tendon which moves across it becomes sore. It is more common in horses over eight years old and initially causes intermittent lameness. Diagnosis is normally by X-ray.

A neurectomy, the cutting of the nerves supplying the foot, is one form of treatment although, like any other type of treatment, it cannot effect a cure once the condition is established. Anti-inflammatory drugs will mask the pain and in recent years the disease has been treated by anti-coagulants, such as Warfarin, which prevent the blood vessels from becoming blocked by clots. This last treatment is usually successful in prolonging the horse's working life.

Pedal Osteitis

This disease occurs as a result of inflammation, similar to that which occurs in navicular, which produces bony outgrowths on the pedal bone. Concussion is a factor in the onset of the disease and lameness is initially intermittent in one forefoot but may become permanent. The condition may be relieved by anti-inflammatory drugs, surgical shoeing or a neurectomy.

Ringbone

This is a form of arthritis. When it affects the pastern joint it is termed "high" ringbone, when it occurs lower down it is termed "low" ringbone, which may or may not affect the joint between the pedal bone and the short pastern. Where the condition affects a joint it will affect the horse's movement and is more serious. It may be caused by concussion, a blow or strain or it may be hereditary. Pain-killing, anti-inflammatory drugs, such as phenylbutazone, may be prescribed or a neurectomy may be recommended.

Sesamoiditis

This is similar to navicular disease except that the bone affected is the sesamoid bone at the back of the fetlock joint. The action becomes pottery and there is little hope of a permanent cure since the disease precludes the neurectomy option. The swelling in the joint may be treated by hosing in order to reduce the pain and anti-inflammatory drugs may be prescribed.

Sidebone

This is caused by an ossification of the lateral cartilages which hold the pedal bone in place, more commonly found in older horses. It may be caused by concussion, bad shoeing, poor conformation or a direct injury. Lameness may be present whilst the sidebone is forming but it usually causes few problems once established.

Splints

Splints are lumps of new bone which form at the junction of the splint and cannon bones on the inside of the foreleg as these bones fuse naturally in a young horse. They are normally caused by concussion and over-working a young, immature horse. The term for the new bone formation is an exostosis. Lameness may be present whilst the splint is forming, in which case rest and cold hosing are recommended, but once formed the splint normally causes no further problems.

Spavins

A spavin is a bony enlargement on the inside of the hock and is an osteoarthritic condition. The usual cause is a strain, particularly in the young horse or one with poor hock conformation. As the condition progresses the horse may become lame but initially lameness may be intermittent, followed by a characteristic dragging of the toe. The lameness may disappear once the spavin has formed but in serious cases it may be permanent or will restrict the horse's work.

Strain Injuries

These usually occur when a sudden and excessive stretch is placed on a muscle, tendon or ligament. The most common tendon strain is that of the flexor tendons of the foreleg, which usually causes heat, pain, swelling and pronounced lameness. Treatment is cold hosing and rest, which may be as long a period as six months for a severe strain. Strained ligaments are less common, cause less swelling and do not normally require a lengthy rest period.

Where a strain occurs in the plantar ligament at the back of the hock it is known as a curb. This is more common in young horses or those with poor hock conformation. Lameness may occur initially but will normally disappear, although the swelling is often permanent.

Bursal Enlargements

These are caused by strains to the membrane surrounding a joint, called the synovial bursa, which retains the lubricating fluid for the joint. The membrane is stretched and fills with fluid, causing a soft swelling. Common bursal enlargements are windgalls, which occur in the fetlock joint, bog spavins and thoroughpins, which occur in the hock and "capped" injuries of the knee, hock and elbow. Bursal enlargements are unsightly but do not normally cause any problems.

Thrush

Thrush is an infection of the tissue around the cleft of the frog which becomes soft and has a thick, foul-smelling discharge. It is caused by bad stable management and may occur in any of the four feet, although more commonly in the hind. In severe cases thrush may cause lameness. Treatment involves cleaning the area thoroughly, where hot tubbing or poulticing may be beneficial, and the application of an antiseptic or astringent, such as Teramycin or hydrogen peroxide.

Punctured or Bruised Sole

These are wounds to the underside of the foot, normally caused by sharp objects or stones. They may be dealt with as normal wounds and may involve the removal of the shoe, depending upon the site of the injury. Puncture wounds to the foot will normally require poulticing to draw out any deep-seated infection.

A puncture may occasionally be caused by the farrier during nailing, when it is called a nail prick. Lameness is normally immediate. Where a nail is driven in too close to the white line, pressure builds up and lameness will occur a few days after shoeing. This is known as a nail bind. Where a bruise occurs between the wall and the bars at the heel it is known as a corn. Corns are usually caused by bad shoeing or leaving the shoes on for too long and should be treated as bruised wounds. Surgical shoeing may be necessary.

Seedy Toe

This occurs when the sensitive and insensitive structures separate and the inferior horn of the white line decays, filling the cavity with a soft, powdery horn. Where this occurs other than at the toe it is known as separation. It is normally caused by dirt getting between the shoe and the foot, causing an irritation, by bad shoeing or as a result of laminitis. The farrier should remove the shoe and the dead tissue and the area should be cleaned by hot tubbing and packed with Stockholm tar and cotton wool.

Wounds

Types

a. Incised (clean cut) — caused by sharp, cutting objects.
b. Lacerated (torn) — caused by barbed wire, nails etc, which tear the flesh, leaving a jagged wound.
c. Contused (bruised) — where the skin is not broken but blood vessels beneath the surface are damaged. These occur as a result of falls, blows or kicks.
d. Puncture — deep wounds caused by stakes, nails or thorns, particularly common in the foot.

As well as accidental wounds there are some which are self-inflicted, normally due to faulty action. These include injuries caused by brushing and overreaching.

Treatment

There are three stages in the treatment of wounds:

    a. Stop the bleeding. Small wounds will normally stop by themselves but if this does not happen then the sides of the wound should be held together. Cold water, which restricts the blood vessels, will also help. If the blood is bright red and spurts out then the injury involves an artery. Direct pressure should be applied to the wound and veterinary assistance sought.

    b. Cleanse the wound. Puncture wounds may need to be poulticed to draw out deep-seated dirt. If there is any swelling around the wound then this may be cold hosed several times a day to help reduce the inflammation.

    c. Dress the wound. Small wounds can be treated with an antibiotic powder such as sulphonamide or an antiseptic spray, such as Teramycin. Larger wounds may need stitching by a veterinary surgeon. Always check that the horse's tetanus vaccinations are up to date.

Stable Vices

Weaving

This is when the horse continually rocks his weight back and forth on his forelegs with his head swaying across the stable door. Serious weaving causes a loss of condition.

   It is thought to be caused by boredom and is virtually incurable. Other horses in neighbouring boxes may also copy the habit. The horse should be kept occupied by giving smaller, regular feeds, haynets etc, and if possible turned out for a period each day. A V-shaped grill fitted to the lower door will prevent the swaying motion.

Crib-biting

A crib-biter grasps the stable door, fence etc with his teeth, arches his neck and gulps in air. This leads to flatulence, colic, digestive disturbance and loss of condition as well as damage to the objects which are bitten. Crib-biters can usually be identified by the fact that their upper incisors will be worn and chipped at the front, making ageing difficult.

Again, it is caused by boredom and so prevention is much the same as for weaving. Painting the woodwork with an unpleasant-tasting substance may dissuade the horse or an anti-crib-biting strap passed around the gullet can be used, which prevents the horse from gulping in the air.

Windsucking

This is the same as crib-biting except that the horse gulps in air without holding onto anything with his teeth. Causes, prevention and remedies are the same as those for crib-biting.

Rug Tearing

Persistent rug-tearers can be dissuaded by fitting a leather or plastic "clothing bib" to the back of the headcollar so that it hangs down behind the lower lip and makes tearing impossible.

Eating the Bedding

The solution is to use an alternative type of non-palatable bedding, after checking for any signs of a dietary deficiency. Shavings or shredded paper are the best alternatives.

13 Equitation

Mounting and Dismounting

Before mounting check the horse's tack. Take note that the saddle is correctly positioned and that the numnah, if worn, is pulled well up into the gullet of the saddle. Ensure that the straps of the bridle are tucked into their runners and keepers and that the throat lash and noseband are correctly fastened.

Check that the girth is adjusted just tight enough to enable you to mount but not too tight. Estimate the length of stirrup by taking the iron up to your armpit. Your knuckles should then reach the stirrup bar with the arm outstretched. Once in the saddle a guide to a general working length is for the base of the iron to be in line with the rider's ankle when the foot is removed from the stirrup and the leg allowed to hang naturally. However, these are only approximate guides. As a rider improves and the seat deepens, a longer length of leather can be used.

To mount, the rider stands at the horse's left shoulder, facing the tail. The reins are shortened to a suitable length and placed, with the whip, into the left hand, together with a handful of mane if required.

The stirrup is twisted clockwise and the left foot placed in it with the toe pointing downwards. The rider turns to face the horse and puts the right hand across the waist of the saddle. The cantle should not be held as this may cause the tree of the saddle to twist.

The rider hops on the right leg, pushing up and straightening the left knee. The right leg is swung over and the rider lowers himself gently into the saddle.

An alternative method of mounting is the "leg up", when the rider stands facing the saddle and bends the left knee so that an assistant can push the left leg upwards as the rider springs from the ground.

To dismount, both reins and the whip are taken into the left hand

and both feet removed from the stirrups. The right hand is placed on the pommel of the saddle, the body inclined forward and the right leg swung well clear of the horse's back. The rider should land gently on both feet beside the horse's shoulder and should keep hold of the reins.

The Rider's Position

The rider sits in the deepest part of the saddle with the weight evenly distributed on the two seat bones.

The upper body should be vertical and held straight, without tension or stiffness. The upper arms hang lightly by the sides, close to the body, with the elbows bent. The wrists should be slightly rounded, the thumbs uppermost and the hands tilted so that each thumb points towards the horse's opposite ear.

The whole leg should be in light contact, the knees relaxed and not gripping. The lower part of the inside of the calves should be touching the horse at, or slightly behind, the girth.

There are two straight lines which can be observed from the ground. The first of these is from the rider's ear, through his shoulder and hip to his heel. This line should be perpendicular to the ground. The second line is from the rider's elbow through the reins to the bit.

The basic position

Holding the Reins

The single snaffle rein should pass directly from the bit, between the rider's third and little fingers, across the palm of the hand and out over the top of the index finger, with the thumb being placed on top of the rein.

The curb rein of a double bridle, normally slightly thinner than the bridoon rein, is held as for a snaffle. The bridoon rein passes round the outside of the little finger, which then divides the two reins.

The Aids

The aids are the means of communication through which the rider's wishes are conveyed to the horse. To a large extent the aids are suggestive — they persuade rather than force and as such are at first used gently, and then with increasing pressure and intensity until the horse responds. The horse then comes to anticipate that stronger aids follow the light ones and will begin to react to the former.

The aids are divided into two groups. The first are the natural aids:

a. The legs
b. The seat
c. The hands
d. The voice
e. The body weight

The second group are the artificial aids, used to support the natural ones. They are:

a. The whip
b. The spurs

The Natural Aids

The Legs

The legs are the driving aids which create energy from the hindquarters. The horse's natural inclination is to move away from pressure by the legs. When both legs are applied at the same time the horse moves forwards unless he is prevented from doing so by a resisting hand when he will rein back.

The legs may be used independently of each other subject to the active leg being supported by the opposite one, in which case the horse will move away from whichever leg is being applied. For example, if the left leg is applied on its own then the horse will move to the right. If both legs are used but the left leg is used more strongly than the right then the horse will move both forward and to the right at the same time. This is the basis for such movements as half-pass and leg-yielding.

The leg should be applied in definite, regular nudges. If there is no response then the aids should be re-applied as before in case the signal was misunderstood or was not clear enough. If there is still no response then a stronger aid may be used, and finally the whip may be used to back up the aid and to encourage a more immediate response.

The Seat

The use of the seat is an advanced aid and is not normally taught to novice or inexperienced riders. However, most riders tend to use their seat subconsciously to some extent. Heavy seats, causing the horse to stiffen and hollow the back, are to be discouraged, the rider being persuaded to let the horse work with minimal influence from the seat. Only when the rider is sufficiently advanced can he expect to use the seat to improve the horse's way of going. The seat can then be used as a driving aid in conjunction with the legs.

The seat is also used to influence the direction of the horse, particularly in lateral work when one seat bone can be weighted more than the other.

The Hands

The hands control and regulate the energy created by the legs and seat and indicate, in conjunction with the body and legs, the direction of movement.

As with the legs, one hand may predominate over the other, but in every instance where a hand acts it must be supported by its partner. The outside hand, for example, controls the speed and helps to maintain the balance, whilst allowing and limiting the bend made in response to the inside hand.

In walk and canter the hands follow the movement of the horse's head, maintaining a light contact. In trot, when the horse's head is relatively still, the hands should also remain still.

The Voice

The voice is an essential training aid, the horse responding to the tone used rather than to the actual words spoken.

In the early days of schooling the young horse the voice, the first aid to be learnt, is used in conjunction with the hand, leg and seat aids until the voice is mainly dispensed with.

On the lunge the voice, in conjunction with the whip, the lunge line and the positioning of the handler's body, is the principal means of control.

Use of the voice, however, is penalised in a dressage test when the horse is expected to be educated to the other aids.

The Body Weight

The rider's weight should be positioned over the horse's centre of gravity as nearly as possible at all gaits. The centre of gravity varies according to the speed and outline of the horse. At speed when the horse is extended it moves forwards. In moments of high collection when the weight of the horse is transferred to the quarters and the base is shortened, it moves more towards the rear.

However, the rider's weight may be used as an aid in many situations, such as in downwards transitions, when the weight sinks down more deeply into the saddle, particularly in the half-halt, as well as being influential in lateral work and when riding turns and circles.

The Artificial Aids

The Whip

The whip is an extension of the leg aid and is used behind the leg to reinforce its action.

There are two types of whip in common use — the long schooling whip, for flatwork and dressage, which can be used without the rider needing to remove a hand from the reins, and the jumping whip which is shorter and thicker and is used for hacking and jumping.

To change a schooling whip from the left hand to the right the reins are taken into the left hand, which is turned so that the whip points directly upwards. With the thumb pointing downwards, the right hand grasps the whip above the left hand. The latter releases its hold, the right hand is twisted to return to normal position and takes the whip in an arch over the horse's neck and down to the right side. The rider then takes the reins back into both hands.

To change a short whip from the left hand to the right hand both reins are put into the left hand. The right hand, thumb uppermost, grasps the whip, pulling it through the opposite hand.

The Spurs

Spurs are used to refine the leg aid and not to strengthen it. They are used in slight, repeated, nudging movements, stroking the horse's sides to obtain a more immediate response to a lightly applied aid. They should never be jabbed into the horse.

Spurs are permitted in all dressage tests but are compulsory at Medium and Advanced levels.

The Gaits

There are four gaits natural to the horse: walk, trot canter and gallop. To meet dressage requirements the first three are sub-divided.

The Walk

A gait of four-time, i.e. there are four distinct beats. The sequence of footfalls is as follows: (i) near hind, (ii) near fore, (iii) off hind, (iv) off fore.

The Trot

A gait of two-time in which the legs are moved in diagonal pairs. For example, the off fore and near hind move simultaneously to produce the first footfall. The horse then springs onto the opposite diagonal, the near fore and the off hind.

The Canter

A gait of three-time. The horse should lead with the right foreleg on a circle to the right and vice-versa. It is termed a "false" lead, or cantering on the wrong leg, when the horse executes a circle to either hand with the outside foreleg leading. The only exception is the more advanced counter-canter when the horse is required to canter with the outside foreleg leading in order to demonstrate a greater degree of balance, suppleness and obedience. The canter is said to be "disunited" when the leading foreleg and the leading hindleg appear to be on opposite sides so that the normal sequence of footfalls is broken.

The sequence of footfalls at right canter are: (i) near hind, (ii) left diagonal, i.e. near fore and off hind simultaneously, (iii) off fore, followed by a moment of suspension.

The Gallop

This is the fastest gait and is generally accepted as being in four-time, although a considerable variation in the sequence may occur according to the speed. As a four-beat gait the sequence is: (i) near hind, (ii) off hind, (iii) near fore, (iv) off fore, followed by a moment of suspension.

Sub-divisions

In school and dressage riding the following sub-divisions are recognised:

     a. Walk: medium, collected, extended and free
     b. Trot: collected, working, medium and extended
     c. Canter: collected, working, medium and extended

A novice horse is only expected to show medium and free walk, working trot and working canter.

Riding on the Flat

In walk the rider's position remains the same as that in halt although there should be a slight following of the movement by the hips and waist and an allowing of the horse's head movement by the hands.

In sitting trot the rider again maintains the correct, upright position,

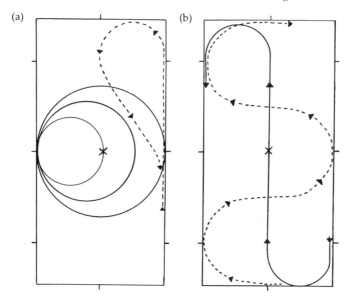

Schooling figures: (a) 10m, 15m and 20m circles; half circle out of the corner, (b) change of rein up the centre line; three-looped serpentine

absorbing the movement of the horse through the back and hips, with the hands remaining still.

In rising trot the rider leaves the saddle as one diagonal reaches the ground and returns to it as the other diagonal reaches the ground. The upper body may be inclined slightly forwards and the hands remain still. On the circle the rider should sit as the inside foreleg (inside diagonal) touches the ground, i.e. as the outside shoulder moves back. The rider should change diagonals by sitting for an extra stride when the direction is changed. To ride constantly on one diagonal encourages the horse to become one-sided, and this should also be taken into consideration whilst out hacking.

At preliminary and novice levels of dressage riders may sit or rise to the trot as they wish but as the horse's training progresses sitting trot is used increasingly and at elementary standard and above sitting trot is obligatory.

During the warming-up period it is advisable to use rising trot to allow the horse time to relax and to avoid the horse's back becoming stiff or hollow.

In canter the rider should stay sitting in the saddle for all three beats whilst allowing the body to follow the movement through the suppleness of the back and hips. There is considerable movement of the horse's head and neck in canter and the rider should allow for this movement with his hands so as to maintain a consistent contact.

Transitions

A transition is a change of pace or a change within a pace. Upward transitions move from a slower pace to a faster pace and downwards transitions involve moving from a faster pace to a slower one. Progressive transitions involve moving from one pace to the next natural one, such as from halt to walk, walk to trot, canter to trot, walk to halt and so on.

A transition from one pace to another out of the progressive sequence is termed "direct", such as walk to canter or trot to halt.

Transitions within a pace are those from one sub-division to another, such as medium trot to extended trot or medium canter to collected canter. At the level of this examination the only transition expected within a pace is for the rider to show a little lengthening or shortening of the stride, most normally at the trot.

All transitions should be preceded by a half-halt so as to rebalance the horse and to prepare him for the change of pace. This is a slowing down of the horse by giving the aids to make a downwards transition but maintaining the leg aid, thus bringing the hindlegs further underneath the horse and lightening the forehand in preparation for a change of pace or direction.

Turns and Circles

On turns and circles the horse's body should be uniformly bent along the line on which the horse is travelling, known as straightness. The smaller the circle or tighter the turn the greater amount of bend required.

The rider should create the energy and impulsion with the inside leg whilst supporting with the outside leg, which prevents the quarters from swinging out. The outside hand regulates the speed and balance whilst supporting and allowing the inside bend requested by the inside hand.

The rider should slightly turn the upper body at the waist so that his shoulders are in line with the horse's shoulders whilst the hips remain in line with the horse's hips.

Outline

The correct outline is one in which the horse carries himself with the hocks well underneath, the muscles along his top line, from the ears to the tail, being stretched and rounded, with the face being carried near, but never behind, the vertical. The outline should remain consistent throughout changes of pace, speed and direction.

To obtain a correct outline the rider should consider the main criteria which need to be established, which are calmness, free-forward movement, straightness and rhythm. The outline will normally follow quite naturally and should never be forced by excessive use of the hands or by the use of schooling aids.

A horse which tends to go with a high head-carriage, has a stiff lower jaw and does not accept the contact is said to be "above the bit". A horse which places the head behind the vertical to evade the contact is said to be "behind the bit" or "overbent". A horse working correctly with a relaxed lower jaw and a calm acceptance of the contact is said to be "on the bit".

Lengthening/Shortening the Stride

Lengthening involves the horse taking longer steps, covering more ground, whilst remaining in the same rhythm and tempo, so that the steps become longer rather than a simple increase in speed. The outline should lengthen, the head and neck will lower as the hindlegs become more engaged to propel the horse along with increased impulsion. The rider should ask for and allow this lengthening whilst maintaining the contact in order to keep the horse balanced and to prevent rushing.

Shortening involves the horse taking shorter steps, covering less ground but again maintaining the same rhythm and tempo. The outline should shorten and the head and neck are raised, lightening the forehand, as the hindquarters lower. The rider should ask for a slower pace by use of the half-halt whilst maintaining the forward impulsion.

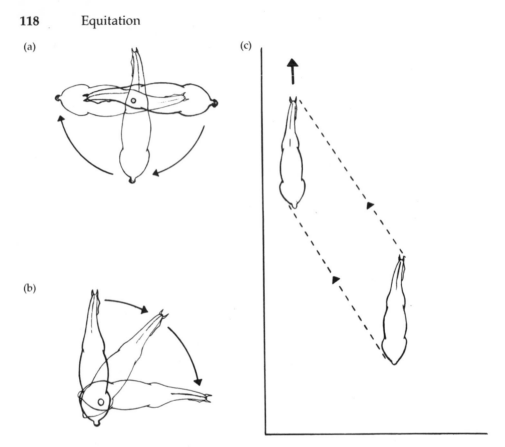

School movements: (a) turn on the forehand, (b) quarter pirouette, (c) leg-yielding

Movements

Lateral movements include leg-yielding, shoulder-in, renvers, travers, half-pass, pirouettes etc.

At this level the rider is required to show the turn on the forehand, some leg-yielding, a quarter-pirouette and the rein back.

Turn on the Forehand

The turn is performed from halt, the horse moving the hindquarters around the pivot provided by the inside foreleg. The turn is named after the direction of bend and not by the movement of the quarters.

If the quarters are to be moved to the right, the left leg is applied behind the girth. The right leg supports in case the horse moves too quickly from the active leg and to prevent the horse from stepping back. The left hand bends the head slightly to the left and the right hand, allowing and supporting the bend, prevents the horse from moving forward.

Leg-yielding

A movement in which the horse moves diagonally, i.e. forwards and sideways, being slightly bent away from the direction of movement, with the body held parallel to the track and the inside legs crossing over in front of the outside ones.

To move from right to left the horse may be taken onto the three-quarter line, the rider's hands are carried slightly to the left without the right hand crossing to the opposite side of the neck. The right leg pushes the horse over towards the track and is supported by the left leg, which also aids in maintaining forward movement.

Leg-yielding can also be carried out on a circle where the horse is asked, for example, to move out from a 15 m circle onto a 20 m circle.

Quarter-pirouette

A quarter-pirouette is performed from walk following a half-halt. It asks the horse to make a turn by moving the forelegs and the outside hind around the pivot of the inside hind.

To turn from left to right, the right rein is opened, the left rein laid against the neck to limit the bend and prevent the horse moving forward. Both hands are carried slightly to the right.

The left leg, behind the girth, prevents the quarters being swung out, whilst the right leg controls the turn. The rider's weight is placed on the outside seat bone by the outside leg pushing further down onto the stirrup iron.

Rein-back

This movement is performed from halt, the horse being required to take two or three steps backwards in two-time, i.e. moving the legs in diagonal pairs.

From a square halt the rider applies both legs to move forwards but has gently resisting hands, blocking forward movement but never pulling back. Equal pressure of both hands and legs should be applied so that the horse steps back straight. When the horse has reined-back the required number of steps, the legs act immediately to obtain forward movement into walk or trot which the hands must allow.

Horse Assessment

When asked to assess a horse after having ridden him, begin by describing the horse. Give the approximate height, the sex, colour, type or possible breeding and the age if it is known. Suggest the use for which the horse would be suitable (hunting, riding school, riding club type) and then assess the way of going. Attention should be paid to details such as responsiveness, obedience, stiffness on a particular rein, temperament (i.e. lazy, fizzy, excitable etc) and performance as it relates to the individual's conformation, i.e. a straight-shouldered horse will find extension difficult. It is also useful to comment on the horse's best, and worst, gait.

The assessment should not be confined to the horse's bad points but should take full account of what is good about him as well.

Riding in the School

For reasons of safety there is set of recognised rules which apply to riding in a school, most of which also apply to riding in an outdoor manège. Riders may work in a group (i.e. as a ride) or in open order (i.e. individually under a previously established instruction, called a "brief"). Lungeing may also be carried out and all three activities can be conducted simultaneously so long as the rules are observed.

   a. Knock before entering the school and wait for permission to enter.
   b. Do not open the door when horses are going past.
   c. Select a safe and suitable place to mount, away from other riders and well away from the track.

d. Pass riders on the opposite rein left shoulder to left shoulder.
e. Allow priority to horses being ridden in faster paces.
f. Class lessons have priority over individuals.
g. Keep clear of any horse being lunged.
h. Horses on the lunge should not impinge on the track.
i. Riders being lunged should be worked in the same direction as the ride to avoid the chance of collision. Riderless horses on the lunge are worked in the opposite direction.
j. Ask permission to leave the school.

14 Jumping

Phases of the Jump

There are five phases to the jump:

a. Approach — The track taken should present the horse at the centre of the fence at the correct point for take off, as dictated by the size and type of fence. As the horse nears the fence the head and neck are lengthened so as to assess its position and size.
b. Take Off — At the moment of take off the horse shortens and raises the head and neck to help lift the forehand as the hindlegs push the body upwards and off the ground.
c. Flight — The horse rounds the back, stretches the head and neck out and down and tucks up the forelegs. As the forelegs begin to extend in preparation for landing the hindlegs are tucked up over the top of the fence. The ideal is for the horse to describe an arc or parabola over the fence ("bascule").
d. Landing — The forelegs are straightened, one meeting the ground fractionally before the other and so momentarily sustaining the entire weight of the horse. On landing the head and neck are then raised to maintain balance.
e. Get-away — The strides immediately after landing during which the horse rebalances himself.

The Jumping Position

The rider's jumping position needs to conform with the phases of the horse's jump. Most riders need to shorten their stirrup leathers so as to close the angles of the hip, knee and ankle joints. The shorter stirrup makes it easier for the rider to incline the upper body forward and

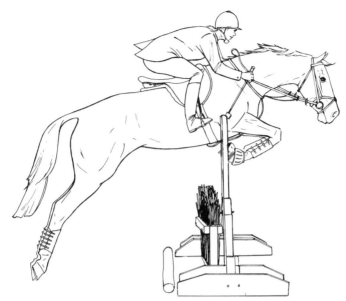

The jumping position.

widens his base of support, which aids balance.

The seat should leave the saddle and move backwards but must remain very close to the saddle. The rider should fold at the hips, rather than at the waist, with a straight back and the head looking forward. The lower leg should remain in contact with the horse's sides with the weight carried through the knee and the ball of the foot to the heel.

The reins are held slightly shorter than normal so that the hands may follow and allow the natural movement of the horse's head and neck whilst still maintaining a contact. The hands should be further towards the horse's mouth but the straight line from the elbow through the reins to the bit should still be evident.

Types of Fences

There are four basic types of fences:

    a. Upright or Vertical—These include gates, planks, upright poles etc, and require accuracy.

    b. Staircase or Ascending—Examples include the triple bar and parallels with the front bar lower than the rear one. These are

the easiest fences for the horse to jump and always incorporate a spread.
  c. True Parallel — Both parts of the fences are at the same height. This is the most difficult type of fence for the horse.
  d. Pyramid — This is where the middle section of the fence is the highest element and the first and third parts are lower, as with a hog's back or tiger trap fence.

Work over Poles

Trotting poles are a valuable exercise, developing calmness, balance and rhythm and promoting muscular development in the horse by encouraging a stretching of the head, neck and back combined with active hock engagement and a consequent rounding of the top line.

They are also an easy introduction to jumping and coloured poles for young horses and for novice riders. To begin with one pole is used, after which three, four or five may be used. The use of two trotting poles is not recommended since some horses may jump them. Trotting poles also provide a useful exercise in balance for the rider.

Placing Poles

A placing pole laid in front of the fence will assist the horse and rider to make the approach correctly and to arrive accurately at the point of take off. It has the effect of adjusting and correcting the horse's stride and allows novice horses and riders to concentrate on the jump itself rather than on "seeing" the correct stride.

Combinations

A combination is two or more fences which are placed a premeasured distance apart, allowing for one or two normal non-jumping strides between each element. In competition a combination will not normally exceed three fences, although more may be used for schooling and gymnastic exercises.

A related distance is two fences placed a pre-measured distance apart, allowing for more than two normal strides between the two fences but arranged for a set number of average strides, such as three, four or five. The larger distance allows for more variation than within a combination, where the number of strides is restricted to that designed by the course builder.

Distances for Poles and Fences

Standard Stride Length on the Flat

	Horse	Pony
Walk	0.9 m (3 ft)	0.8 m (2¾ ft)
Trot	1.2 m (4½ ft)	1.2 m (4 ft)
Canter	2.7–3.6 m (9–12 ft)	varies according to size

Trotting Poles

	Horse	Pony
Trot Distance	1.3 m (4½ ft)	1.2 m (4 ft)

Placing Poles

	Horse	Pony
Approach in Trot	2.7 m (9 ft)	2.4 m (8 ft)
Approach in Canter	5.4 m (18 ft)	4.8 m (16 ft)

One Non-jumping Stride between Fences

	Horse	Pony
Approach in Trot	5.4 m (18 ft)	4.8 m (16 ft)
Approach in Canter	7.3 m (24 ft)	6.4 m (21 ft)

Two Non-jumping Strides between Fences

	Horse	Pony
Approach in Trot	9.7 m (32 ft)	9.1 m (30 ft)
Approach in Canter	10.3 m (34 ft)	9.4 m (31 ft)

Bounce (no stride between fences)

	Horse	Pony
Approach in Trot	3.0 m (10 ft)	2.7 m (9 ft)
Approach in Canter	3.3 m (11 ft)	3.0 m (10 ft)

Note: where there are more than two elements to a combination the distances for one and two non-jumping strides would be slightly longer between the second and third elements (and any further elements) than those figures given above which are distances between the first and second elements. Similarly, if a combination comprises a spread followed by a vertical it may be necessary to increase the distance by up to 0.3 m (1 ft).

15 Teaching in Theory and Practice

A Good Instructor

An instructor should be enthusiastic, self-confident and patient. Teaching requires a knowledge and enthusiasm for the subject coupled with an ability to get along with people and good communication skills. A good clear voice is essential, preferably one which is interesting and easy to listen to.

The instructor needs to be alert and well able to spot faults and quickly but positively correct the pupil in an encouraging but never patronising manner. Tact and self-control are of the essence.

The ability to explain clearly and demonstrate where necessary are vital to the improvement of the pupil, as is an awareness of each individual rider's particular needs.

The instructor needs to be constantly aware of safety whilst teaching and to have a strong sense of responsibility. It is important to act as a professional at all times. This includes having a smart appearance and a sympathetic but authoritative manner. A sense of humour is a definite advantage.

Principles of Good Instructing

The following points should be noted:

    a. Plan lessons beforehand and have a logical long-term aim for each pupil which is geared to gradual progress.

    b. Give instructions clearly and with sufficient warning.

    c. Have an experienced rider as leading file.

    d. Keep your eyes on the whole ride all the time, not merely on the individual executing an exercise, in order that con-

126

trol of the ride may be maintained and dangerous situations avoided.

e. Introduce exercises which will benefit all riders, beginning all new exercises in walk first, and gear the lesson to the most novice rider in the group.
f. Assess progress regularly and share your attention equally.
g. Be sure that all the riders understand each exercise before commencing and encourage them to ask questions.
h. Never begin the next rider on an exercise before the previous rider has finished.
i. Give criticisms positively and in an encouraging manner.
j. Give frequent, short rest periods.
k. Aim for the riders to enjoy their lesson and end on a good note.

Improving the Pupil

A thorough assessment of both horse and rider are the primary concerns. The instructor should establish the level and ability of the horse and rider, their age, fitness, temperament, aims, main strengths and weaknesses etc. These factors will influence the method and manner of instruction.

After an initial discussion rider assessment is best made by observation. Observe the relationship between horse and rider. Is the rider dominating or a passenger? Is he quick to correct the horse, perhaps too quick? Does he ride accurately and with sufficient forward movement? Does he have sufficient contact or ride with more hand than leg? Is the horse happy or tense? Is he going forward willingly or is he unsettled? Is he attentive or "switched off"?

Most positional problems fall into two categories—stiffness and crookedness. These are normal postural problems for most people which may become more pronounced on a horse. Beginners, unfit or nervous riders are more likely to suffer from stiffness whilst crookedness may affect anyone. The instructor should be aware of the rider's physical make-up, such as build, weight, etc, and the way in which this causes particular problems.

Children are less well able than adults to concentrate for long periods so exercises should be short and varied, designed to keep the pupils' interest and attention. Exercises which are fun as well as educational are more likely to encourage concentration in younger pupils who will learn more in consequence.

Use of the Voice

The ability to project the voice clearly requires practice. Pupils who cannot hear instructions will inevitably remove some of their concentration from their riding in straining to listen. Face pupils when speaking and confine yourself to one spot, suitably chosen.

Words should be spoken slowly and care taken not to miss letters from the ends of words or to slur words into each other. Air should be projected out of the diaphragm rather than from the throat as this will eliminate the need for shouting and preserve the voice, enabling the instructor to teach for longer periods without discomfort.

Lesson Structure

a. Introduction—Introduce yourself (first name only is sufficient) and then go to each rider in the class, asking their name and checking the fitting of the horse's tack.

b. Explanation—Define the objectives of the lesson and the type of exercises you intend to set.

c. Demonstration—Demonstrate personally only if really essential, otherwise use the most experienced rider in the class if a demonstration is necessary.

d. Warming-up—Spend ten minutes getting horses and riders settled with simple exercises.

e. Instruction—This is the work period during which the instructor must have the complete attention of the class so as to put the lesson across and it will take up most of the allotted time.

f. Conclusion—Revise the main points of the lesson. Give praise where it is due and point out general, individual problems. Be positive and always encouraging. Consolidate the work done and check on pupil assimilation by asking questions.

g. Invite Questions—Encourage pupils to ask questions and answer them honestly and accurately.

Safety

The emphasis put on safety in all aspects of work can never be too great. In a teaching environment it is the responsibility of the instructor to ensure that the lesson is as safe as it is possible to make it.

Accidents, by the very nature of the unpredictability of horses, will happen but in many cases they can be avoided by common sense and forethought.

The following points may be noted:

  a. Observe the rules for riding in a school at all times.
  b. Ensure that the horses' tack and the riders' attire are safe.
  c. Halt the ride for taking away, adjusting or taking back stirrups.
  d. Check that riders maintain pace and distances.
  e. Remove disruptive horses and place them at the rear of the ride.
  f. Never use two trotting poles as horses can be inclined to jump them.
  g. Remove jump cups from wings when not in use and do not allow riders to jump towards a ride working at the other end of the school.
  h. Never ignore a problem until it becomes out of control.

A thorough knowledge of the BHS accident procedure is essential, and any accident should be entered into the Accident Book.

16 Lesson Requirements

The Class Lesson

The first part of the Preliminary Teaching Test is the class lesson. This requires the candidate to take a group of horses and riders (normally three or four) for approximately 20 minutes and to teach a given subject. They will normally have half of the school to use as another candidate will be teaching at the other end, with the exception of some, though not all, jumping lessons. It is important that everything the riders do is safe.

The list of class lesson subjects (known as "briefs") which may be set for an exam is extensive. The following is a selection of the subjects which the candidates may be asked to undertake:

    a. Warming-up the horse and rider.
    b. Improve the ride's work at sitting (or rising) trot.
    c. Improve the ride's work at canter.
    d. Teach mounting, dismounting and give suppling exercises to improve the ride's position.
    e. Teach turn on the forehand.
    f. Improve the ride's understanding and application of the aids through transitions.
    g. Give a lesson involving the use of trotting poles and also explain their use to the class.
    h. Teach leg-yielding.
    i. Give the ride their first jumping lesson.
    j. Work the ride with reins but without stirrups in walk, trot and canter.
    k. Teach the ride to show a few lengthened strides in trot.
    l. Teach the ride to perform quarter-pirouettes.

Suggested Content of Class Lessons

The following are guidelines for two of the above class lessons. These are for guidance only and may need to be adjusted according to circumstances, space and equipment available, ability of the horses and riders etc. At all times stick rigidly to the brief you have been given and avoid spending too much time warming-up or getting side-tracked onto other problems.

Warming-up the Horse and Rider

Introduction

Explanation — Both horses and riders need to warm up and relax as well as having time to settle and get used to each other. Warming-up is to settle the horse and supple both horse and rider.

Demonstration — None necessary.

Instruction — Suggested exercises: allow the horse a long rein to stretch his neck and top-line, riders remove feet from irons to stretch the leg (walk only), work in rising trot (less strain on the horse's back than sitting), work on turns and circles, forward movement and lateral suppleness, canter work, suppling exercises for the rider (in walk first).

Conclusion — Most effective methods of loosening up horses involve circles and canter work; for riders suppling exercises and relaxation. Warming-up is essential before more intensive work can be undertaken.

Invite Questions

Give the Ride their First Jumping Lesson

Introduction — Check that all horses are fitted with neck-straps.

Explanation — Explain correct jumping position, use of coloured poles as an introduction to jumping and how to ride over a single fence from trot.

Demonstration — Ask a pupil to move in front of the ride and place him in the correct jumping position, pointing out the main considerations.

Warming-up — Brief flatwork using turns and circles.

Instruction—Suggested exercises: work over one, then three, trotting poles, encouraging straightness and correct approach, use one placing pole to a small cross pole (halt the ride and send each rider out individually if space is limited), then raise the fence to a small upright if all riders are confident.

Conclusion—Reconfirm the jumping position and the way to ride a single fence. Point out individual problems and give encouragement and praise where due.

The Lead Rein Lesson

Candidates will be expected to take either a lead rein lesson or a lunge lesson. Normally one lunge lesson will take place at one end of the school and two or three lead rein lessons at the other end. Both lessons will be on a one-to-one basis (i.e. you will have only one pupil).

The lead rein lesson will normally involve a pupil who is a beginner, who may be nervous and who will not be riding fit. The duration of the lesson will not normally exceed 15 minutes.

Structure of the Lead Rein Lesson

Introduction—In the exam the horse and rider will normally be in the school ready for the candidates. The instructor should introduce himself and ask the candidate's name and riding experience. The horse's tack should be checked, the instructor explaining what he is checking as he proceeds and encouraging the pupil to check the tack himself. The horse should wear a neck-strap and a lead rein, which should be fitted through the near-side bit ring and attached to the off-side one.

Explanation—Much of the lead rein lesson will consist of constant explanation as situations arise but initially the instructor should explain how to tighten the girth and adjust the stirrups, getting the rider to do these things for himself. The instructor then explains the way to mount.

Demonstration—The instructor should demonstrate the way to mount and dismount and the correct basic position adopted in the saddle.

Warming-up — None necessary.

Instruction — The rider should mount with assistance and encouragement from the instructor. The position is adjusted and the instructor needs to explain how to hold the reins. The rider should be shown how to adjust the stirrups and to check the girth.

The aids to walk and halt should be explained before the rider is asked to move off. The position may be continually corrected, with the instructor leading the horse, and the rider may be instructed in making simple changes of direction.

Trot may be attempted after an explanation of the aids and the rider can be encouraged to try rising to the trot, counting aloud the one-two rhythm. The pupil may be allowed to hold the pommel of the saddle with the fingers of the outside hand.

Little more is possible in the time allowed and the lesson should normally be brought to a close with the pupil dismounting, running up the irons and taking the reins over the horse's head in preparation for leading the horse back to the stable.

Invite Questions — The rider should be encouraged to ask questions throughout the lesson as well as at the end.

The Lunge Lesson

The lunge lesson in the examination will be confined to 15—20 minutes. Candidates will not have to give a lunge lesson as well as a lead rein lesson. The pupil will be either a novice with some experience or someone a little more advanced who is working towards HK & R Stage II.

Structure of the Lunge Lesson

Introduction — Ask the pupil's level of experience.

Explanation — Explain the objects of lungeing and give an assurance to the pupil that control is the responsibility of the instructor.

Demonstration — None necessary.

Warm-up the Horse — Do this in the pupil's presence to demonstrate your control over the horse. Circle briefly on both reins without the side-reins and then with the side-reins attached.

Warming-up — Remove the side-reins for mounting and reattach them once the rider is settled in the saddle. Work the horse and rider at walk and trot with reins and stirrups.

Instruction — Have the pupil knot the reins and drop them on the horse's neck but never allow the reins to be out of the rider's reach. Work at walk and then at trot, introducing simple rider exercises. Once the pupil is confident ask him to quit and cross the stirrups, crossing the right one first and pulling the buckles away slightly so that the leather lies flat under the rider's thigh. Quitting and retaking the stirrups should always be done at halt.

Begin all exercises in walk first, then repeat at trot. The pupil may lightly hold the pommel of the saddle with the fingers of the outside hand until he is sufficiently confident to release the hold. Change the rein regularly, both to work the horse equally and to enable the instructor to correct the rider from both sides, always giving the rider warning when you intend to change pace or direction. The rider should take back the stirrups and have a short period of rising trot before the session ends. Ensure that the knot in the reins is untied and side-reins detached before the pupil dismounts.

Conclusion — Reaffirm lunge objectives. Indicate the progress made and areas where more work is needed.

Invite Questions

Exercises on the Lunge

The following are examples of exercises used on the lunge to correct postural faults and encourage suppleness:

    a. Arm circling — circling the arms backwards, individually or together, brings the shoulders back and releases tension.
    b. Circling the head — releases tension from the neck.
    c. Shrugging the shoulders — releases tension from the shoulders.

d. Touching the toes—individually or both at the same time, encourages suppleness in the waist and hip joints.

e. Rotating the ankles—releases tension from the ankle joints and helps to open up the hip joints.

f. Lifting the leg away from the saddle, stretching it down and back and then returning it to light contact—helps to deepen the seat and places the leg a little further to the back of the saddle.

g. Swinging the lower leg—increases mobility of the knee joint and makes the lower legs more independent.

h. Rotating the upper body by holding the arms outwards at shoulder level and rotating the body to the left and right so that the arms are parallel with the horse's spine whilst the hips remain facing forward—increases suppleness in the waist.

i. Swinging the arms backwards and forwards—encourages better posture and releases tension in the shoulders.

j. Deep breathing exercises—relaxes the rider and deepens the seat.

k. Stretching the body upwards with the arms extended whilst stretching the legs downwards—deepens the seat and straightens and lifts the upper body.

l. Swinging the body backwards and forwards to lie on the horse's quarters or neck—encourages suppleness in the waist and hips. To be performed only at halt or walk.

Lead Rein Versus Lungeing

Opinion is divided as to whether beginners are best taught on the lead rein or the lunge. Both methods have their advantages and disadvantages.

On the lunge the pupil can concentrate entirely on the position, leaving control to the instructor and can thus establish a good basic position before taking control of the horse himself. The instructor is able to see both horse and rider more easily and can correct positional faults more accurately. However, the pupil may be inclined to feel more nervous and insecure by the distance away that the instructor is required to stand and though it is possible for the rider to develop a more secure seat he will learn nothing about control.

Conversely, the lead rein method inspires confidence and a closer teaching situation with a greater degree of supervised control. The beginner rider, however, has then to think about both his position and the horse and the instructor is less able to see the horse and rider as a whole by being too close and may at times have to resort to walking backwards.

A sensible compromise would be to start the pupil with two or three lead rein lessons to build up confidence and then go on to lunge lessons, alternating the two as required.

17   The Five-minute Lecture

Candidates are required to give a five-minute lecture on a set subject. Ample time is given for preparation but notes are not permitted. The audience will normally consist of the remaining candidates and the lecture should be aimed at HK & R Stage II or Pony Club C standard.

Preparation

Plan the lecture around a few salient points and have to hand any "props" (such as grooming equipment, feed samples etc) which you may be able to use to improve the clarity and quality of the talk. Time the lecture to cover a little over rather than under the allotted time.

Delivery

Begin by introducing yourself and defining the lecture content. Deal clearly with each specific point in a logical order. Speak up, speak clearly and do not hurry. On conclusion invite questions.

Lecture Subjects

The following is a selection of subjects which candidates may be asked to cover. Subjects are confined to stable management and general care and will not involve riding or teaching theory.

    a. Preparation of boiled feeds
    b. Uses of a haynet
    c. Preparations for clipping

d. The grooming kit and its uses
e. Watering in the stable and at grass
f. Care and cleaning of tack
g. Stable construction
h. Roughing off
i. Prevention of worms
j. Turning out of ponies after lessons
k. Responsibilities of late-night duty
l. Basic rules of feeding
m. Fire precautions in the yard
n. Yard safety
o. The riding and road safety test
p. Conformation
q. The medicine cabinet and its contents
r. Boots and bandages
s. Preparations for transporting a horse
t. Care and maintenance of a paddock
u. Isolation procedure
v. Qualities of good bedding
w. Types of fencing—advantages and disadvantages
x. Types and uses of rugs
y. Care of indoor and outdoor schools
z. Riding on the roads

18 Teaching Format

The Examination Discussion

The Teaching Format section of the examination takes the form of a discussion among the candidates in which the examiner will participate by asking questions and adding comments.

The examiner will usually set up an imaginary situation and invite candidates to make comments, observations or suggestions.

The subject matter varies considerably and will often include theoretical questions about the principles and practices of teaching. A sound knowledge of theory is therefore essential but it is also necessary for candidates to have a wide experience of practical teaching if they are to contribute positively to the discussion. It is not advisable for candidates to become argumentative or to present themselves as being too dogmatic.

Teaching Format Questions

The following are examples of the types of discussion subjects which might be encountered. However, the subject matter is so variable that these questions should not be taken as being actual questions for this section. They do, nevertheless, offer an example of the sort of questions likely to be posed.

1.   You are going to give a beginner his first lesson:
   a. What would you advise the client to wear?
   b. How would you go about instilling confidence in the client, assuming that he has had no previous contact with horses?
   c. What factors should you consider when teaching a complete beginner?

  d. Would you prefer to lunge your client or to give him a lead rein lesson, and why?
  e. How would your lesson differ if your client was a child?

2. You are going to give a lunge lesson to a novice adult:

  a. What qualities would you look for in your lunge horse?
  b. What would you hope to achieve by lungeing this rider?
  c. What exercises would you give this rider?
  d. How can you ensure that the lesson would be safe?

3. You are taking a more experienced rider for a jumping lesson:

  a. What type of horse would you like for this client?
  b. How would you warm up the horse and rider?
  c. What exercises would you use before beginning to jump?
  d. How would you improve the rider's jumping position?
  e. How would you help the rider overcome any nervousness about jumping?
  f. How would you ensure that the lesson was safe?

4. Do you consider an indoor school to be vital for teaching novice riders?

5. What qualities would you look for in a good riding school horse for a novice rider?

6. What do you consider to be the qualities of a good riding instructor?

19 Examination Format

The Examination Day

If possible visit the examination centre before the day and find your way around. It is permitted for candidates to take the examination at a centre at which they have trained but this is not the case at BHSII level and above.

Make sure that you are suitably dressed. A well-fitting hacking jacket with cream or beige jodhpurs or breeches and long, black boots are preferable, together with a white shirt and suitable tie or a correctly tied stock.

You must wear a current BSI hard hat or crash cap with fitted chin strap and ladies should wear a hairnet where appropriate. You will need a schooling whip for flatwork and a short whip for jumping and you should wear gloves at all times, especially whilst riding, leading and lungeing. Avoid excessive amounts of make-up or jewellery.

For the Teaching Test you will need a BHS Log Book and for all examinations a notebook is advisable.

Present a professional appearance at all times, being courteous and polite. Join in the discussions where possible but avoid being too dominant. The attitude of a candidate may be considered in borderline cases.

Horse Knowledge and Riding Stage III Timetable

The Horse Knowledge and Riding Stage III examination and the Preliminary Teaching Test are normally held on separate days. The following is an example of the type of timetable which might be expected on a Stage III examination day. It assumes that there are 13 candidates:

8.30am		arrival at examination centre
8.50am		introduction by chief examiner and distribution of numbered armbands to candidates
9.00am	candidates 1—6 candidates 7—13	flatwork minor ailments paper
9.45am	candidates 1—6 candidates 7—13	minor ailments paper flatwork
10.00am	candidates 1—13	jumping
11.30am	candidates 1—6 candidates 7—13	lungeing and ride and lead first aid
12 noon	candidates 1—6 candidates 7—13	first aid lungeing and ride and lead
12.30pm	candidates 1—6 candidates 7—13	oral stable management oral/practical stable management
1.30pm		lunch
2.30pm	candidates 1—6 candidates 7—13	oral/practical stable management practical stable management
3.30pm	candidates 1—6 candidates 7—13	practical stable management oral stable management
4.30pm		results, individual discussion between examiners and candidates

Preliminary Teaching Test Timetable

The following is an example of the type of timetable which might be expected on a Preliminary Teaching Test day. It also assumes that there are 13 candidates:

8.30am	arrival at examination centre
8.50am	introduction by chief examiner and distribution of numbered armbands to candidates

9.00am	candidates 1–6	class lessons
	candidates 7–13	teaching format
10.00am	candidates 1–6	teaching format
	candidates 7–13	class lessons
11.20am	candidates 1–6	lunge or lead rein lessons
	candidates 7–13	five-minute lectures
11.50am	candidates 1–6	five-minute lectures
	candidates 7–13	lunge and lead rein lessons
12.20pm		results

Note: sufficient time is allowed after the teaching format sessions to prepare for the five-minute lecture.

20 Horse Knowledge and Riding Stage III

Flatwork

Candidates are required to ride three horses. One of these will be ridden without stirrups. Much of the section is spent working in open order to a given brief. For example, the candidates may be asked to work on turns and circles in order to assess the suppleness of the horse. A simple change of leg through trot at X may be required.

Jumping

Candidates are asked to jump a small course of fences (up to 0.9 m/3 ft) on two different horses. The course will comprise six to eight fences and will include a double (normally one-stride) and a related distance (i.e. two fences with three, four or five strides between them). The first fence may be used as a warm-up or practice fence.

Oral Stable Management

This section covers feeding, stable construction, bedding, care of stabled and grass-kept horses, fittening and roughing off, care of the hunter or competition horse, horse physiology, horse psychology etc.

Oral/Practical Stable Management

This section will be held under practical stable conditions and includes clipping, the foot and shoeing, conformation etc.

Practical Stable Management

Candidates may be expected to demonstrate bandaging, preparation for travelling, saddlery fitting and condition, plaiting, grooming etc.

Minor Ailments Paper

A written paper consisting of five questions to be answered in 45 minutes.

Lungeing

Two candidates share the school and will be required to demonstrate lungeing an experienced horse for exercise. Duration is approximately 15 minutes.

Ride and Lead

Candidates need to demonstrate their ability to ride and lead in a simulated road situation and are expected to mount and dismount with two horses unaided.

First Aid

This section is very brief and involves simple questions about the Highway Code, Country Code, basic first-aid and accident procedure.

Results

Results are made known within an hour of the examination being completed. Candidates are given a pass, a "borderline" pass or a fail for each section and likewise for the overall examination. A "borderline" pass indicates that further work is needed on particular points within a section. Candidates who fail the first-aid section but otherwise obtain a pass may still be granted an overall pass if able to produce a valid first-aid certificate.

21 Preliminary Teaching Test

Class Lesson

Two candidates will share the school and will be expected to take three or four pupils, teaching to a given brief.

Lead Rein/Lunge Lesson

Three lead rein lessons may be carried out at one end of the school whilst one lunge lesson occupies the other end.

Five-minute Lecture

This will normally be held in the tack room or office and candidates will address the audience, normally consisting of other candidates in the same section, in turn.

Teaching Format

This discussion will normally take place in the tack room or office and will last approximately 30–45 minutes.

Results

Results are made known shortly after the end of the examination and individual discussions with examiners may take place. Successful candidates will receive a pass slip from the chief examiner.

Whilst the British Horse Society Assistant Instructor's Certificate is a professional examination and the examiners have a responsibility to ensure that high standards are maintained, the examiners do want candidates to pass and will give assistance and advice where possible in a friendly and sympathetic manner.

The examination day should not be looked upon so much as a test but more as an opportunity for the candidate to demonstrate his knowledge and skills. The examiners will be aware of candidates' nervousness and may often overlook the odd mistake provided that the candidate shows an acceptable standard over all.

Try to relax and enjoy the day—it will not be as bad as you expect. The AI exam is a qualification worth having and will undoubtedly teach you skills which will be useful in other areas of life. The satisfaction of becoming "qualified" makes all the hard work worth it. I wish you every success in your endeavours.

22 Recommended Reading

The BHS publishes a list of recommended reading for the examinations:

Equitation   BHS
Horse and Stable Management   J. Houghton-Brown & V. Powell-Smith
Levels of Horse Care and Management Books 1 & 2   BHS
The Manual of Horsemanship   BHS
Riding and Road Craft   BHS
Rule Book for Dressage   BHS
Principles of Riding   German National Equestrian Federation
Advanced Techniques of Riding   German National Equestrian Federation
Foaling: Brood Mare and Foal Management   Ron & Val Males
Getting Horses Fit   Sarah Pilliner
Horse Business Management Reference Book   P.L. Cross & J.H. Brown
Training Showjumpers   Anthony Paalman
Transporting Horses by Road   BHS

Note: all candidates should be in possession of a BHS Log Book.

Index